IMPOSED ID_.
AND BRITISH FURTHER
EDUCATION

Dr Javeria K. Shah

IMPOSED IDENTITIES AND BRITISH FURTHER EDUCATION

The experiences of learners classified as "low ability"

The Education Studies Collection

Collection Editor
Dr Janise Hurtig

Copyright © 2022 Javeria K. Shah

British Library Cataloguing in Publication Data
A CIP record for this book is available from the British Library

ISBN: 9781915271150 (pbk)
ISBN: 9781915271174 (ePDF)
ISBN: 9781915271167 (ePUB)

The right of Javeria K. Shah to be identified as the Author of this work has been asserted by her in accordance with the Copyright, Design and Patents Act 1988.

Cover design by Fiachra McCarthy
Book design by Rachel Trolove of Twin Trail Design
Typeset by Newgen Publishing UK

Lived Places Publishing
Long Island
New York 11789

www.livedplacespublishing.com

In loving memory of my dear friend and creative genius, Jennifer Williams-Baffoe, who left the world a little sadder on 19 March 2022. Thank you, my sister ally, for the conversations, the love, the solidarity, and the memories. Never forgotten.

Abstract

This book amplifies the stories of young people classified as "low ability" by drawing on the author's "person-centred" research into the long-term impacts of "low-ability" classifications on young people's academic performance and journeys beyond school. The study traced "low-ability" learners from the starting point of their vocational media Further Education (FE) journeys with a deliberate focus on eliciting learner voice and experience – alongside staff perspectives on systemic barriers to learning, teaching, assessment, and opportunities for classified learners.

Young people classified as "low ability" share in their own words their stories of negative school experiences, the impact of being classified, and experiencing vocational media education in FE while labelled as "non-academic". Different learner accounts reflect larger issues surrounding their social classifications, and how they navigate intersectional identity amid their own identity formation.

This book brings the voices from FE that are usually omitted from educational research by providing direct insights into the narratives of young people classified as "low ability" in their own words over a sustained period. In doing so, readers are given insights into the lived experiences of young people who have been negatively classified while at school and the impact this can have on their self-identity formation, lived experience, quality of learning, and academic/professional outcomes.

Keywords

Low-level learners, negative classifications, learner experience, media education, vocational training, Further Education, socialised identities, GCSE failure, low-ability learners, learner journeys

Contents

Acknowledgements

I would like to acknowledge every first-generation immigrant's dream, as reflected in the hardships that my parents endured so that I could receive a "British Education". I am grateful to my father for fostering a family environment that values ideas, ethics, and debate, and my mother for her continued support and encouragement.

I wish to thank my MA Education Consultancy family for the safe spaces, the encouragement, and support in bringing the counter narratives to the forefront. I am so grateful for you!

I add acknowledgement and thanks to the Further Education sector and to former colleagues, comrades, and students. Thank you for the memories – I have walked away with a strong pedagogy and a resilience that is serving me well.

This book is dedicated with love to my daughter, Arrisa – you can achieve anything!

Introduction

This book is based on a ten-year-long research project that I conducted in an English Further Education (FE) college that I will be referring to as "South College". During this research, I spoke to young people classified as "low ability" and FE staff who shared their lived experiences of studying and working in FE. Shared experiences that helped me understand the impact that negative categorisations can have on learners and the role that FE staff may consciously or sub-consciously play in reinforcing or challenging this status quo.

This research was inspired by my experiences of learning and teaching in the FE sector in the UK. My time in FE was instrumental in helping to shape my teacher identity as an activist educator committed to recognising the power and agency of a learner to generate their own meanings and truths. To affirm that learners aren't empty vessels to be filled, or passive participants in education: that they are and should be active agents within an educational framework of respect, dignity, and equality. These values ran across all aspects of this research in the shape of "person-centred" approaches and continue to inform my teaching to this day.

During my time in FE, I noticed that there were significant changes being made to the level 2 (General Certificate of Secondary Education (GCSE) equivalent) qualification landscape, as well as continued policy changes. Some of these changes included a shift from the creative GCSE retake options in the 1990s to a primarily vocational equivalency model in the 2000s; especially the introduction and withdrawal of the General National Vocational Qualification (GNVQ) and the implementation of the Business and Technology Education Council (BTEC). Alongside these changes, I noticed a division between "academic" and "vocational" at level 2; a division that was much stronger than when I had been an FE learner. As an FE media lecturer, I also noticed that vocational level 2 learners were being marginalised in the classroom because of negative classifications such as "low ability", "learning difficulties", or "behavioural issues" and were often steered into lower-level vocational media qualifications. This made me wonder if these learners knew how they were seen and categorised. I also questioned the impact of negative classifications on these learners' life chances. The more I thought about it, the more I questioned the role of level 2 vocational qualifications in the lives of negatively classified learners. I wanted to know more about:

- The experiences of negatively classified learners in their own words;
- The impact of negative classifications on learners;
- Whether educators and institutional management shared the same vision of the learning, teaching, and support they were providing young people; and
- Whether teaching staff were equipped and adequately supported to deliver specialist courses such as media studies.

Motivated by the premise that lived experience is not uniform across society, and that our sense of social reality in all its classifications is constructed, I spent ten years trying to find the answers to my questions. In doing so, I gained valuable insights into the young people in this study, in their own voices. I learnt about their personal and academic struggles, their school contexts, their sense of self, until I left them after a decade as young adults in a world very different to the one at the beginning of the project. I kept the people in this study as my focus throughout and created a person-centred approach.

Person-centred research can be characterised by its inclusion of individual subjectivities that are treated as an intrinsic part of an inquiry (Biehl, Good and Kleinman, 2007). This type of research aims to develop holistic understandings that can only be achieved through access to the personal truths of those affected by what is being researched (Quinney, 1982; Woodward, 2017).

The value of subjective experience and personal truths was the strength of this project. Furthermore, the presentation of individual voices without editing or reinterpretation was an additional strategy used to ensure that participant narratives were presented as close to how they were shared. The ideological framework that underpins this study is nuanced in its focus and considers the various elements that make up the human experience within education structures.

Marx *et al.* (2017) observe that education mirrors society and its hierarchies of privilege and marginalisation and that lived experience and personal stories can highlight individual impacts of these hierarchies. The positioning of the educational institution as a reflection of society challenges the educational researcher/ practitioner to make sense of their lived experiences within the broader praxis of the educational space (Elbaz-Luwisch, 2010; Fraser, 1997; Frost *et al.*, 2010).

This book returns to my study to delve deeper into the experiences of young people and staff to identify how inequality can play out in the British education system – but also with a purpose to tell the stories that may not otherwise be heard. Stories of negatively classified learners and stretched FE staff in their own words.

I have used aliases for the college and all individuals to maintain anonymity and have framed each chapter with learning objectives so that readers can take something tangible away for their practice and reflections. Finally, this book is my parting gift to FE, as I try to bring the voice of the individuals within the system to broader discourse on policy, education, and the FE sector.

1

The Further Education policy context

This chapter sets out the South College landscape that the young people were studying in, as well as introducing the English FE sector that South College is a part of.

Learning objective: Understanding the FE landscape

- To facilitate a broader awareness of the FE landscape and the significant part that policy plays in defining the sector and its provision.
- To enable broader awareness of the crucial part that FE plays in supporting diverse learner groups.
- To raise awareness among FE decision makers on issues surrounding the employment of unqualified sessional staff and the potential negative impacts of this on learners.

Understanding the English FE sector

The sizeable FE landscape differs widely in its provision and blend of funding organisation and channels (Briggs, 2005; Lingfield, 2012). The sector offers provision to 14-plus, adult, lifelong, and community learners in the shape of vocational and general education, short courses, higher education (HE), and apprenticeships and hosts diverse learner groups of all ages and experiences (Corbett, 2017). Bathmaker and Avis (2005) aptly profile the FE learners as

> [f]ull-time students, workers and trainees doing part-time off-the-job learning, mature students returning to learn, people taking night classes, learners following individualised study programmes, as well as groups of students learning in the community.

> (2005, p. 8)

Figures released by the Association of Colleges (AoC) in 2017 reported that the sector was servicing 2.2 million people, including 16,000 14–15-year-olds and 712,000 16–18-year-olds that were enrolled into 280 colleges of which 186 identified as FE colleges (Association of Colleges, 2017). AoC figures also reported that the average college trains 1,200 apprentices and, in 2017, 77,500 16–18-year-olds were recorded on apprenticeships with a global figure of 313,000 students on apprenticeship provision in colleges (*ibid.*). The report also stated that 1.4 million adults were studying in colleges, of which 151,000 people were studying higher education in a college (*ibid.*). In 2015/2016, sector income totalled £7 billion (*ibid.*). These figures support assertions from

Norton (2012), who states that the diverse English FE sector plays a crucial role in servicing its local, regional, and national communities with lifelong learning opportunities.

The FE sector is frequently positioned as a second-chance provider for 14–19-year-olds (see Foster and Park, 2005; Hodgson and Spours, 2017; Mehaffy, 2012; Tolland, 2016) – and is recognised for the positive role that it plays in the academic development of the secondary failed learner (Department for Business Innovation and Skills, 2015).

> Students whom no one else wants to teach, namely, those who have failed to gain five good GCSEs at the age of 16, and, through sheer hard work and through forging more respectful and inclusive relationships, (FE) restore(s) them as human beings who begin to see themselves again as worthy of respect and who can and do succeed in gaining qualifications.
>
> (Coffield *et al.*, 2007, p. 724)

While some have acknowledged the role of FE as crucial in supporting and developing students that have failed in the mainstream system (see Appleby and Bathmaker, 2006; Department for Children, 2008; Hayward *et al.*, 2005; House of Commons Education Committee, 2011), there are others that have problematised the positioning of GCSE failed learners in FE on predominantly low-level vocational courses and questioned the credibility of GCSE examinations as a "reliable indicator of achievement" (Sheerman and Silver, 2013, p. 24). For example, the Nuffield Review of 14–19 Education and Training in 2005 reported that GCSE-failed learners belonging to low socio-economic groupings were mostly attracted to low-level vocational courses in FE and challenged the assumption that learners achieve general qualifications based on ability. The Review stated that "the struggle to renew students' interest in learning does not get reflected in the values implicit within the tables by which providers are judged – even though 'social inclusion' is at least formally an aim of government policy" (Hayward *et al.*, 2005, p. 196).

Despite a substantive remit, FE is often identified as the Invisible Man or Cinderella to account for its perceived marginalised status (Hyland and Merrill, 2003; Norton, 2012). Steer *et al.* (2007) and Atkins (2009) have cited both the nature and frequency of educational policy change as accounting for FE's marginalised status.

FE and policy

Many have acknowledged the challenges for FE in implementing ambitious policy changes with ever decreasing funding (see Ainley and Bailey, 1997; Hayward *et al.*, 2005). A 2015 survey conducted by *FE Week* revealed disaffection among FE staff due to funding cuts, a singular apprenticeship government focus, and an increase in retake maths and English GCSE offer. The report stated that

> there was a clear sense from everyone in the follow-up survey that government reforms will have unintended and damaging consequences. These reforms appeared to be based on little or no evidence, it was viewed – if impact assessments had been carried out, they hadn't been communicated to the people interviewed.
>
> (Burke, 2015)

The article concluded that,

> despite the determination of everyone to provide a professional and effective service, the deep cuts and contradictory policy demands will inevitably hit learners – with the most disadvantaged being the worst affected. Provision to school leavers who – through no fault of their own – fail and need the help of FE will almost certainly deteriorate.
>
> (*ibid.*)

Connecting the demands made on the sector with a lack of funding represents policy expectations that could be argued as ambitious and unrealistic (Hayward *et al.*, 2005). Begging the question: how will FE lecturers be able to successfully guide learners to qualifications over one academic year, when the same learners were unable to achieve these qualifications after 11 years in the schooling system (Burns, 2014; Wolf, 2011)?

14–19 policy

During the time of this study, 14–19 educational reform was a crucial backdrop to the FE lives of staff and learners and some of the young people in this study had their first exposure to South College aged 14. FE and school partnerships featured strongly in the 14–19 reforms as a means of co-facilitating vocational training. However, findings from Rose in 2012 concluded that "school partnerships were less defined in their approaches and were often characterised by informal, personal and ad hoc processes" (2012, p. 88). Comparatively, Haynes and Lynch (2012) noted that cross-sector collaborations were "loose" for level 2 and, while demonstrating that the "key elements" were in place, still reflected a "limited drive", being at their "strongest" for level 3 (2012, p. 438). Moreover, Hillier (2006) argued that some schools were exploiting the framework to achieve positive data and pass off students that were found troublesome or at risk of disengagement. These assertions were supported by Burgess *et al.* (2010).

A teacher survey conducted by the National Union of Teachers and University College Union in 2012 substantiated this picture by concluding that

> 14–19 education and training is a complex, turbulent and sometimes bewildering area of education to work in for teachers and lecturers and that there is often no settled will on key aspects of national policy.
>
> (Hill *et al.*, 2012, p. 29)

Sector shifts were underpinned by New Labour's emphasis on challenging issues of parity of esteem between vocational and academic. This involved an aim on the government's part to enhance vocational choice and excellence by shedding vocational education's identity as a "sink option for failed students" and aimed to attract the "bright and able" to applied courses (DfES, 2002, p. 4). Some, such as Hillier (2006) and Haynes and Lynch (2012), problematised the access to opportunity for learners classified as low ability in their appraisal of the reforms. It has been argued by some that the 14–19 framework has promoted a plethora of middle-track qualifications (Hodgson and Spours, 2008) that have potentially compounded the marginalisation of young people most likely to undertake them (Atkins and Flint,

2015). This discourse has highlighted an "unintended" (Hodgson and Spours, 2009, p. 6) policy-levered marginalisation of second-chance learners. Atkins (2013) has supported these assertions by extending FE's invisible identity to the low-level vocational learner.

Media educationalist David Buckingham has described the 14–19 reform as "one of the most misconceived and expensive educational disaster stories of recent times" (2017, p. 32). He positions this within the context of a still complex vocational landscape that he ascribes to "policy hyperactivity" (*ibid.*, p. 27).

Given the demise of the diploma system, it is possible to conclude that the only functioning legacy of these reforms is the continued inclusion of 14-plus learners in FE, which, according to Elwood (2013), is shaped though a range of discrete partnership programmes that are no longer representative of the nationwide policy-driven narrative.

FE and the creative arts

In 2010, a coalition between the Conservative Party and the Liberal Democrats replaced a New Labour government and policy focus was moving away from the 14–19 vocational strategies in favour of new reform (Young, 2011). The change in government led to a notable shift in policymaking with a marked emphasis on "academic rigour" (House of Commons Education Committee 2011, p. 61), marked by reforms to the national curriculum, a reduction in GCSE/A Level re-sit opportunities and the launch of an English Baccalaureate (EBacc). Policy emphasis on the value of academic subjects demonstrated a notable omission of the arts, including media studies, which are often classified as soft subjects (see Hayward *et al.*, 2005; O'Connor, 2000; Ofsted, 2010; White, 2013). Hodgson *et al.* (2017) assert that the policy-driven "erosion of the Creative Arts subjects" (2017, p. 36) reflects a lower status for the Arts. Buckingham (2017) has asserted the challenges in locating low-level vocational media education in FE. An appraisal of the literature supports these findings and reveals a knowledge gap in the positioning of media education in FE policy frameworks. This can also be connected to the generally marginalised status for arts disciplines under recent policy reforms (Dennis, 2016).

Some have also problematised the position of the media lecturer in the context of a conflicted identity for media education in a digitally evolving world (Buckingham, 2007; Shah, 2017). This prompts us to question whether this identity for the discipline is negotiated in digital contexts where the learners are often identified as digital natives and may demonstrate a higher technical aptitude than their teachers (Shah, 2017; Buckingham, 2011).

Framing vocational education and training (VET) within the praxis of market-led policy rhetoric leads to a discussion on the positioning of industry training and exposure within the qualifications. Alongside Wolf (2011), some studies have also problematised the quality of industry contexts to vocational training. For example, findings from a study conducted by James (2002), which focused on the GNVQ teaching experiences of a Business Studies lecturer, concluded that learners demonstrated a "source of tension" because of the "tenuous links between the course and eventual employment (and) students felt that a business studies qualification should lead directly to a good job" (2002, p. 400). The study concluded that learners felt disaffection at learning that their business "course had no work experience provision and there was no clear progression route into employment" (*ibid.*).

In his appraisal of the Creative and Media Diploma, Buckingham (2017) highlights the lack of media industry/employer input into the generation of these diplomas. Although Buckingham (2017) recognises some positive media teaching to have emerged from within the short life span of the diplomas, he concludes that broadly speaking the diploma was unsuccessful due to an insufficient balance of vocational and academic focus (2017, p. 37). Buckingham (2017) observes that in recent years there has been a notable increase in the disciplines vocational and higher education offer, which, although positive for the status of the subject, has also been problematic in respect to the increase in graduates requiring media employment in a competitive industry (2017, p. 32). Educationalists have continued to argue that media education remains removed from industry (see Buckingham, 2007, 2017; Buckingham and Scanlon, 2005; Kirwan *et al.*, 2003; Thornham and O'Sullivan, 2004), rasing questions in connection to the recruitment of young people onto media courses. What attracts GCSE failed learners to GCSE-equivalent media qualifications? What do they hope to achieve because of undertaking media qualifications? Are young people taking these courses to enable educational progression or access to the industry?

In a study including BTEC level 2 and 3 creative media students in FE, Atkins and Flint (2015) claimed that learners had joined their courses by "serendipity" (2015, p. 35) and asserted that

> [r]ecent 14–19 policy, structured around models of instrumental or technical rationality (Hodkinson et al., 1996, p. 120; Wright, 2005, p. 9), mistakenly assumes that all young people have the ability, support and understanding to make an informed rational and unconstrained career choice from an almost infinite range of possibilities. The data from this study disputes this.
>
> (ibid., p. 45)

Framing media education into this, it is possible to argue that some learners may be entering media courses in FE without sufficient information on what the subject involves and subsequently how their course may benefit them in the future.

In summary, while the decisive role of FE as a second-chance provider is widely acknowledged in the literature, educational discourse suggests a complex and often transient FE landscape because of the policy process, often acknowledging a disconnection between the rhetoric and reality and asserting a policy-levered instability and inequality to the sector. Others have criticised the lack of local actor inclusion and evidence-based approaches. Taking this criticism of educational research into consideration, I chose to develop a person-centred research approach that would address the lack of voices.

2
Meet the staff

In this chapter, we meet South College staff who provide insights in their own voices into how they were navigating learning, teaching, and management within and beyond the college and, consequently, how this may have impacted the young people in this study.

Learning objective: Policy enactment

- To invite educators to interpret national and institutional policies in ways that centralise learner advancement and progression.
- To motivate education leaders to engage in holistic decision making which incorporates staff consultation and considers student wellbeing as well as long-term impacts.

Meet the principal

David Saunders held the principalship of South College from 2009 to 2011. As part of the interim management team, David held the post while the college was stabilised in preparation for the appointment of a permanent principal.

> I was asked to come down and meet with the college because the challenge that South College presented required an experienced interim manager, and it was thought that I was the most appropriate person to come into the role. Usually, I would have sent one of my team in, but because of the situation South was in, it was felt that I ought to come and take the role on.

South College was David's first principalship. Before this, he had accumulated a range of experience in the business and education sectors. David drew parallels between himself and the typical FE student when recalling his former, mostly unsuccessful, academic career (Bathmaker and Avis, 2005; Hillier, 2006).

> Not unlike a lot of our students we get, I hadn't done as well as I could have done at school and hadn't got the qualifications. I hadn't gone onto college or university when I could have done when I was younger.

The impact of David's school failure on his lack of progression into further and higher education is indicative of the influence that academic failure holds over a learner's educational life path and trajectory. In drawing parallels between his earlier academic failure and the typical FE learner, David acknowledges that FE attracts a high proportion of learners that have failed at school. This supports the idea of FE as a provider of second chances for GCSE failed learners. David's lived experience enables him to recognise the value of FE for learners that have failed in their secondary education, hence placing him to be empathetic towards the GCSE-failed learner in FE.

David's post-school journey comprised acquiring industry experience in the business and advertising fields and returning to study at his local FE college as a mature student.

> I seized the opportunity, went back to college as a mature student, and went to my local college.

David's transition from study to industry exemplifies sector practice that positions the failed secondary learner as vocational (Wolf, 2011). David's self-identification as a "mature student" indicates that he spent significant time in industry before returning to study in FE. David's shift into FE represents a period of personal change and uncertainty.

> Picked up a business studies course, found it pretty easy, then moved onto an HND programme, did a HND, topped up the degree. And during that time when I was studying, I thought I'd like to work in education and in fact I'd like to teach, because I'd always been interested in training. A couple of people encouraged me and I went and talked to a Head of Department and said, "look you know if I was going to be a teacher, what do I need to do to get to that place to be a teacher?" So we talked and I went off and did it, and fortunately I was lucky to get a job in the very same college, my college that I'd started off. I worked initially in the library at the college and started doing a bit of part-time teaching and that snowballed.

David's movement between various courses and employment within his FE college echoes findings from a study by Atkins (2017), which looked at the career and course decision-making processes of young people and concluded that young people's vocational trajectories and transitions implicated a "serendipity" (2017, p. 642) in learners' decision making and choices. A serendipitous dynamic also features in David's "snowballing" metaphor for his transition into teaching. David's FE college clearly played a crucial part in enabling him to retrain and change professional direction.

> I was very lucky [with] my first college, it was and is, still is, an outstanding college, and I was fortunate enough to start my time in FE now with them. Teaching snowballed in terms of quantity eventually to the stage where I was appointed as a full-time lecturer, then into middle management and eventually I left that college after a number of years, moved into a senior management role.

David's FE story represents an inclusive FE environment that successfully supported him through significant professional change and indeed awarded him a second chance. However, David's story is underpinned with a counter narrative of hard work and perseverance on his part. He sheds light on these features of his personality and talks about the ambitions that took him away from his college.

> I'm very ambitious and I knew that staying in the southwest of England was not adequate enough in terms of career, in terms of me being able to develop, so I had an offer from a few associates to work with them as an interim manager, and that's taken me to a number of colleges through that time. I've worked in sort of

> East London, Essex, er, in the north of England, North London, among other places and you get a variety of experiences. My role with the company currently is as Managing Consultant, so I lead the curriculum team.

David recognised the limitations of the college and transitioned into an FE management consultant role. The shift is indicative of a possible lack of broader opportunities for ambitious staff in FE. David's reference to the regional location of the college also suggests a perceived link between geographical areas and access to opportunity.

Meet the experienced media lecturer

Connor Mills joined the South College media department as a sessional (hourly paid) lecturer in 2001 from industry and was made a permanent member of the team in 2004. Connor's pre-South College trajectory shared notable similarities to David's in that, like David, Connor had also represented a serendipitous path (Atkins, 2017).

> I have a varied career path and have worked as a branch accountant for a fruit and veg company, a credit controller, bank cleric, and courier, but following an extensive time travelling around the world, my aim was to save and work my way through a broadcasting degree as a mature student. Following that I began a career in local radio with the BBC. This I continued for 10 years (predominantly on a freelance and part-time basis) [and then] I effectively fell into teaching.

Connor's entry into media education through industry represents the vocational teaching dynamic in FE, which includes trained/trainee lecturers and non-teacher-trained industry practitioners. This dynamic has been both encouraged and challenged in wider debates. While one angle to this has put emphasis on the pedagogic value of the trainee teacher and considered the tensions of training and teaching in FE, another aspect has challenged the lack of industry practitioners teaching on vocational courses (see Department for Business Innovation and Skills, 2014; Wolf, 2011). Colin joined South College as teacher training was becoming a mandatory requirement for teaching within the sector. To continue teaching at South, Connor undertook an in-service Postgraduate Certificate in Education (PGCE). An experienced member of the teaching team, Connor was regarded as a level 1 and 2 specialist, although he also taught on level 3 programmes such as BTEC and A Level media.

> Joined South College as a sessional in April 2001; started PGCE in 2003; became FT [full time] in 2004. Started by teaching solely radio production skills although this was soon expanded into more theoretical areas including A Level classes.

Connor's emphasis on A Level as "theoretical" is indicative of the broader divisions between vocational and academic (Bell and Stevenson, 2006). The distinctions made by Connor are indicative of the style of teaching that he would have carried out in his academic and vocational classes.

Meet the new teacher in training

Michael Pinaccetti joined South College in 2007, some years after graduating in fine art. Initially in a departmental support role, he transitioned into the college's in-service PGCE programme in 2009. Like David and Connor, Michael's move into teaching had come later in life. Experiences of failure formed a significant part of Michael's retrospections, and he shared primarily negative experiences of secondary school.

> I generally found secondary school quite negative. It culminated in my last year [with] my GCSEs [not] being as positive as I thought [they would be]. The outcome was very poor! This was sort of pre being statemented for learning difficulties in schools or colleges. So I think the general assumption was that I just perhaps … not stupid but just had limited abilities and was seen as a challenging student. Like for instance now there would be support put in place, if they could see someone was struggling. Dyslexia isn't just about writing; you know it could be other things. I struggled through a lot of subjects and could have benefited from more support. Even the subjects where I did do well in, such as art … um I was seen as being too slow.

Michael attributes his poor GCSE results to his dyslexia and to the lack of support he received at school. However, he acknowledges that his dyslexia was unidentified at the time and links this to an unsupportive approach to learning difficulties in the 1990s. It is possible to situate Michael's experiences of specific learning differences (SpLD) and GCSE failure within broader literature, which draws connections between GCSE failure and special educational needs (see Association of Colleges, 2017; Hayward *et al.*, 2005; Waterman, 2011). Post-secondary, Michael struggled with feelings of low self-esteem. He attributes this to a lack of college and family support.

> My parents were trying to encourage me not to do art, even though they could see that was what my main passion was. While my college was telling my parents, "We advise him perhaps to, even though he has some skills, to go on somewhere else". It didn't help my confidence at all.

There is a clear connection between Michael's dyslexia and interest in art and, later, in media. These two elements in his learning narrative represent a familiar association between students that gravitate to art/media and the presence of a specific learning difference (Tobergte and Curtis, 2013). Furthermore, Michael's positioning as a dyslexic learner, classified as "slow", is representative of broader discourse, which connects SpLDs, GCSE failure, and low academic ability. Sharing similarities with the learners in this research, Michael moved into a level 2 vocational programme after failing his GCSEs. The vocational shift in Michael's early academic trajectory reflects policy discourse, which identifies a pattern of GCSE failure leading to vocational transitions.

> The level 2, erm, was interesting because there was only five of us to start with, two people dropped out, there was three of and we our teacher [sic] at the time was very much a schoolteacher. He had a very traditional

approach to teaching, which I struggled with. That was his approach, very strict harsh criticism, and a way of forcing you to reassess your mistakes. I didn't respond very well for a very long time to this, but it did get me through the course. We had to do a final major project. I specialised in African art and that was where I got the merit, before that I was scraping by. So that last few units I picked myself up and did well.

The challenges described here represent Michael's continued lack of academic confidence and a lack of engagement with "school style" teaching. Michael's personal development had been negatively impacted by his GCSE failure and subsequent lack of support from within his immediate environments. Despite his negative experiences of teaching and learning on the level 2, Michael reflects positively on the level 2 in the context of his higher education.

[The level 2] did give me some grounding later on with studying photography and digital imaging at Reading. It gave me that sort of almost a technique, instilled the techniques in me, yes.

Following an alternative route into higher education, Michael successfully completed a range of vocational courses, including a foundation degree, before enrolling on to a bachelor's degree at a specialist art school. Michael's routing into vocational courses at levels 2, 3, and 4 indicate that he was classified by the school system as a "practical learner" rather than academic. Michael's academic trajectory can be argued as supporting findings from Wolf (2011) and Atkins (2013), which assert predestined vocational pathways for learners perceived as low ability. As Michael shares here, after failing at GCSE, it was felt that "anything practical or non-academic was the only option". Michael's story embodies the deeply entrenched division between academic and vocational education, which has been argued as positioning vocational learners as destined for manual trades and the academic learners suitable for entry into the professions. Michael's comments also capture the damage that this division often does to learners' self-esteem and, subsequently, academic self-concept.

> I mean now I have a very clear idea of what being academic is, I don't have a fear or disdain for academia, and I can appreciate it. I think at the time I felt because I did so poorly that I would never participate or be associated with anything that was academic, perhaps more so in terms of writing or theorising, you know applying the theory to the practical. I felt I would become [sighing] at best an engraver, rather than an artist, art critic, journalist, or designer.

By the time Michael progressed onto a foundation degree at Reading he was beginning to critique his academic self-concept of being a vocational learner destined for the trades.

> Reading was very closed off and it was very technical, very competitive. I am interested in the technique, in the technical aspects but that's only a part of it. I knew if I went down that route I would be a technical photographer. You know, only interested in the technique rather than the approach or the aesthetics.

Michael opted out of the degree top-up option and chose to pursue a photography apprenticeship for a brief period. Through the apprenticeship, he was able to gain broader industry exposure and became interested in joining a specialist London-based art institution. This was in part because he wished to pursue a more holistic, creative training, which integrated theory and practice and was not purely technically orientated.

> After Reading, I opted out of the BA conversion at the last minute and did a bit of industry experience. When I was in the industry, those people [were from] St Martins or one of the big London institutes [and] were explaining to me how open it was. So, I applied and got into a London art school. I was intrigued by what it would be like to be part of a London institute.

Michael's emphasis on shifting from an outer London higher education institution to a London-based institution echoes the connections that David makes between opportunity access and geographical locations. It is possible to say that Michael was able to appreciate his disciplines because of the learning that took place out of the classroom in the shape of his work experience. It is also possible to conclude that Michael's exposure to industry was a crucial factor in enhancing Michael's confidence, aspirations, and academic self-concept.

Staff perspectives on FE and South College

FE as a second-chance provider for failed learners

David defined the sector as providing second chances to failed learners and celebrated the work carried out in FE. His summary of what the sector does connected with his own experiences of second chances in FE.

> I think FE does a wonderful job with lots of young people because they go into a system for 11 years, they come out at the end of it having failed. We get them for a year, maybe two if we're lucky and we're expected in that very short period of time to turn them around, to get them to achieve what they failed to achieve in 11 years. So you know when you step back and look at it you think well actually we do a bloody good job on the whole.

David identifies a vocational function for FE in servicing the failed learner. David's emphasis on BTECs as an alternative for failed learners reflects a focus on the sector's vocational strengths and is indicative of a vocational positioning for the GCSE failed learner. It could be counter-argued that distinctions between school as sites for academic study and FE for vocational reinforce the historical problem of the lack in parity of esteem between an academic and vocational provision that Atkins (2009) has identified.

The key for me is what's gonna be different about somebody coming to a college that means they will achieve compared to what they've just gone through. BTECs offer I think that difference and it allows us to offer a difference which means that people that haven't got five A stars to C can achieve something which it is the equivalent of.

David raises an important point regarding the failed learner. If after 11 years in the school system learners have failed, what can FE offer them that they have not experienced already? Furthermore, what can FE do with the same academic provision that they have failed in, in a shorter period of time? This resonates with what I discussed in Chapter 1 regarding policy-levered shifts towards compulsory maths and GCSE retakes in 2011 and connected issues concerning GCSE retakes in FE. Leading me to ask: if a GCSE retake framework is not suitable for FE or the failed learner, then what options do these learners have apart from vocational level 2 courses?

The FE sector's marginalised identity

Both David and Connor identified the sector as having a marginal status, concluding that FE was "forgotten" by policymakers in comparison to the school and higher education sectors.

David: The school sector is sacrosanct, no governments are gonna really squeeze the school sector, they'll do it subtly, but they won't do it openly … and HE, while it's had a squeeze recently, is still better funded, better thought of than the FE sector. So yes we will continue to be the sort of forgotten sector, I think we'll always be that sort of almost like a naughty child sat in the corner …

Connor: The story has now been told but FE in my opinion has always been the forgotten sector and a forgotten institution with no money, it is a dark and difficult place to thrive.

This view of the FE sector as marginalised is not unique to these members of staff. As I discussed in Chapter 1, FE's low status has been frequently discussed in the broader literature. The experience of diverse and complex academic histories among the people I interviewed enabled them to understand the sector in more ways than most. Staff shared a nuanced relationship with the sector that predated their professional teaching involvement. The FE learner had become the FE teacher, hence generating a multi-layered awareness of the sector that entwined lived experience and professional contexts. At its best, this shared background (between staff and students) held the potential for the collaborative and supportive learning relationships which mark the positive FE experience. However, the percolation of policy-levered changes inevitably affected the ecology of South College. David reflects on the leadership rationale and processes that underpinned a period of restructuring and redundancies at the college, which made an impact on level 2 media learners' teaching and learning.

Uncertainty and change

David: The hard decisions are when we start to look at redundancies and restructuring and people losing jobs. That is very difficult. You know you don't ever want to put people in a position where they're gonna have to leave the organisation or they're gonna lose their job, but you have to because actually it's for the good of the college. Ultimately that's gonna have an impact, positive impact on the student experience. So those are hard decisions, but you do what you think is absolutely right. You know once you've done that you have to stick by that and stay with it and I'm absolutely sure that the decisions we've taken are right. People that have left the organisation or changed jobs and it's had an impact on their life. I understand that thoroughly, but you know what we're doing is right. You know the decisions around the management structure and keeping the SFC site and A Levels and all the other bits and pieces, I think that's the right thing to do. Key now is that the college has got to step up and everybody in the college has got to start stepping up and saying actually you know we're gonna make this a better place.

Framing David's reflections ecologically, a rippling impact effect can be identified in the way this dynamic disrupts the media department and the level 2 media learners' experience. David's reference to the individuals within the college reflects an attempt to empathise with staff that have been negatively affected by the changes. There appears to be a tension in David's response. On one hand, he empathises with the individuals affected by his decision making, while, on the other, he adopts a leadership persona encouraging the college community to overcome the problems they have experienced to "step up". It is possible to infer from this that, in David's view, the college community has been lacking the drive required to stabilise the college.

Comparatively, Michael's reflections indicate feelings of uncertainty among learners and suggest learner vulnerability in a regulatory and provisional sense. Echoing the concerns I cited earlier in this chapter, David also problematised students undertaking English and maths GCSEs in FE, when they had already failed this provision at school and in most cases were often on level 1 and 2 courses.

> Can we meet the demands and the expectations of the schools and what they want? How will those impact upon us? So there's been lots of discussions going on there – but we have taken the view that we're gonna need to increase our GCSE maths and English re-sits. So you've got people that are coming level 1/level 2 and we're saying to them well you've got still to do your GCSE maths.

David also shared concerns about the weight of this provision on FE and how this may affect an already challenged sector.

> I think the question I suppose is, what can FE do? If we simply mirrored a school system where we said actually if you've not got your five A stars to GCSE, you come to us and do a broad GCSE programme ... what's gonna be different? What can FE do differently often in a year with those GCSE students that they didn't do at school? That means that they will achieve as opposed to them not achieving GCSE and that's the age-old issue with maths and English retakes you know ... okay, I didn't

get my C, A to C in maths and English, so therefore I'm
gonna redo it at college. Well okay, but what's gonna
be different? I mean … you know, what can the college
do that's gonna mean that you can achieve it and what
can you do as an individual student that can mean you
can achieve it? I'm always a little bit worried that there's
just this assumption that we do it and, therefore, and
everything will be wonderful …

Policy pressures

David's primary concern in connection to the expansion of
offering maths and English re-sits in FE seemed to primarily
link to a policy-driven agenda to potentially steer FE towards
mirroring what schools do, but to do so in a year – and, hence,
conflict with his views on a specialist vocational identity for FE
that is distinctly different to schools, questioned earlier in the
chapter. On the theme of rapid change, Michael also reflected
on the changes in the BTEC qualification structure.

It keeps changing, I was up to date on it and, but we've
just received a report that suddenly informs that the
assessment is going to change, so I'm afraid I'm not that
knowledgeable on that at the moment.

There appears to be a unanimous view that there is a lack of
coherence in government policy towards FE when connecting
the lived experience of the staff in this study with the broader
literature discussed in Chapter 1. Which brings me to funding.

The FE funding framework is regarded as a critical challenge for
the sector, because of its complexity and limitations. As the FE

remit continues to expand to the "everything else sector" (Allen and Burgess, 2010, p. 1), colleges are challenged to achieve more with less. South College Principal, David, captures the dynamic of demands on the sector to achieve more with less, in his summary of funding cuts to the sector under the then newly formed coalition between the Conservative and Liberal Democrat parties.

> There's the cut in funding that we have experienced, which we described as dubious, because if you say to the man in the street, or they've cut entitlement funding, nobody understands that. So it's just gone under the radar, nobody's noticed it but you know in financial terms for a college like this that's a million pounds of money gone out the door. Yet we're still expected to do the same as we were doing before. There's a perception we've had five or six good years. And I don't think we've had good years. I think we had five or six okay years. But there's a perception that now we can squeeze it back a bit more.

David draws attention to policy assumptions that the FE sector has had a good run under New Labour funding policies. In challenging these assumptions, he represents the view of management and leaders on the FE ground and highlights divisions in the lived experiences of those working in FE and policymakers. David projects continued tensions between FE and policymakers under the coalition.

> It's gonna get harder and more challenging or difficult as time goes on, money is no doubt gonna be tighter,

you know every year we're expected to do more for less or more for the same money.

David's predictions of a policy-levered decrease in funding and an increase in expectations of performance are not a unique projection for the sector. In a report published by Engineering UK two years after David's interview, Kumar *et al.* (2013) concluded there would be continued funding cuts to the FE sector.

FE will have to do more with less. Funding for FE will decrease over the next two years: in 2012/13, the investment in adult FE and skills will be £3.8 billion, dropping to £3.4 billion in 2013/14 and £3.3 billion in 2014/15.

(2013, p. 78)

The report also revealed shifts to funding frameworks in line with government priorities. Perhaps the most concerning feature of the FE sector's ambivalent funding dynamic is its potentially negative impact on teaching and, subsequently, the learner experience – linking to issues surrounding the negative impacts of funding mechanisms on an institution's ability to strive for learner-centredness and maintain high-quality standards.

Since 2011, when David was last interviewed, the FE sector has experienced several funding reforms; however, it could be argued that funding frameworks are not so much the problem as a complicated and transient system.

David captures this complexity in his summary of the coalition government's reform to funding bodies.

One of the areas that I really feel is wrong and wasteful

is the split we've now got between YPLA which funds 14 to 19 and the SFA which funds everything else and then in fact you've got HEFCE as well with HE. So, on a simple level, we are dealing with three separate funding bodies, which creates challenges, difficulties, and extra work for us as a college. In my view this is wasteful of the public purse and overly bureaucratic and complicated – because you have three quite large organisations operating to fund one relatively small sector. I'm concerned that we are an easy target for a squeeze and that that will continue.

David highlights a complicated and inefficient tripartite funding framework, which creates a bureaucratic burden for the college. Moreover, David's concerns relating to the sector within a new policy dynamic capture a continued perception of policy marginalisation among staff. David's views on a complicated FE funding model were supported in the Wolf Report (2011), released in the same year as his interview.

The system is complex and completely opaque to the vast majority of those working within the system, let alone the public at large. It imposes very large administrative costs on institutions; and, as basic economic or management theory would both confirm, opaque systems are also intrinsically inefficient and subject to extensive gaming.

(2011, p. 120)

Where is the information?

While David suggested a lack information access in respect to policy and change management, Connor identified an internal information deficit. It is possible to conclude that the lack of information flow produced a disruption across the top tiers of the South College ecosystem. At grassroots level, Connor and Michael's responses suggest that the South College environment was not conducive to effective media teaching and learning, as both lecturers highlight issues surrounding departmental leadership and management and college and departmental information flow.

Further to restructures and redundancies, the media department had lost its subject-specific management structure. The media team felt marginalised due to a loss in a media-specific management presence and in becoming a subsidiary of the Creative Arts and Design Faculty. This was epitomised by Connor's remarks, which emphasised a lack of media-specialist representation with the management team: "Most importantly (there is) no departmental managerial representation". Geographically distanced managers were unable to provide the department with the sustained leadership and support that it required. This dynamic exacerbated tensions within the department as established staff felt excluded from departmental-wide decision making and unsupported due to the absence of a media-specific manager. The restructure became a catalyst for radical behavioural and cultural shifts within the department. As staff felt marginalised, they disengaged from departmental concerns, retreated from collegiate working, and focused narrowly on their own teaching.

A fractious infrastructure

Somewhat ironically, in the meantime, Connor was sharing his management aspirations with relevant leaders and expressing a strong desire to take on management responsibility of the media department. Expressions of interest from Connor did not come to fruition and subsequently reinforced his feelings of disaffection.

> I also feel robbed of any prospect of career progression within a management structure now so small and coterie filled. I have consistently requested training in management systems over many years and it has been noted on my appraisal and I have consistently been overlooked.

The absence of a curriculum and middle management infrastructure and high staff turnover had negative impacts on the team. Connor summarised the shift in the management culture within the department through using the platform of the departmental meeting: "These have changed from friendly and supportive with time allocated to team meetings that are too often confrontational, non-supportive, and lunchtime meetings". The emphasis Connor puts on the negativity experienced in team meetings and their lunchtime scheduling reflects resentment towards shifting college dynamics, which contradicts David's feelings that the college was improving in its culture and practices.

Staff on the ground, such as Connor, were expressing a very different experience. Michael's experiences correlated with Connor's to some degree. When retrospectively reflecting on his knowledge of working within the media team between 2009 and 2011, Michael identified some of the critical issues that he had observed in the early years of his teaching career within the media department.

> I'm afraid to say the department itself felt quite fractured and fragmented with people sort of diverging off into different areas. We could have pooled our resources together a bit more, which at the time would have made me feel a bit more reassured. I felt it was a collection of individuals, which was a bit disconcerting, and you could if you weren't careful find yourself on your own.

Michael's observations of a department filled with "individuals" reflected the emerging culture at South College, post-merger, which appeared to be shifting towards a more atomised, anomic culture. This was perhaps a subconscious survival mechanism to cope with the rapidity and subsequent uncertainty at the college. Furthermore, the pressures of achieving "good data" were beginning to shadow the emphasis on teaching and learning, as Michael notes here:

> I was particularly disappointed last academic year when we had to assure our senior management that we would get two BTEC level 3 students through and get a hundred per cent success rate. There was very little (student) disciplinary measures put in place. Management were ridiculous, pathetic and inadequate, in fact if they were to be graded, they would be 4. The students are aware of this, the students know about this, the students utilise Facebook and Twitter and any other online social source to share this. So that, that puts us

in a weak position, a vulnerable position, an unhealthy position. I feel that also leads to a greater struggle to, to get them through when certain students have taken full advantage of that. We have unfortunately lost a number of students who, that are more than capable, who clearly have very good creative skills, some in animation or some more with the writing and now are in low-end jobs you know.

Problems in the media department

It appears that while management was mediating broader institutional policies, the media department was operating under expanding accountability. According to Michael, this dynamic seems to have been noticed by social media savvy learners who were using their digital networks to criticise the department. Michael also draws attention to issues surrounding learner behaviour, classroom management, and insufficient student disciplinary framework as barriers to learning and teaching within the department. Michael's account implies that learner dissatisfaction was arising from a lack of learning and teaching quality and that this was reflecting in learners' retention and negative assessment outcomes. This suggests a lack of strategic direction for the college, increased pressures, and a problematic infrastructure, subsequently causing negative impacts on learner experience. Furthermore, Michael's experiences suggest marginalisation of staff and learners within South College.

Michael shared his uncertainties for the future of the department given its internal special measures status.

> I was worried the department might be closing down. Statistically the numbers weren't very positive. It's diabolical that we haven't been told. We were on special measures partly because of these low stats rates. I'd like to think we're not on special measures anymore, I'd love it if someone actually mentioned that we're not, that would be somewhat professional. The positives are I think we are actually now doing better than we were.

The theme of insufficient information reflects strongly on Michael's response as he queries the special measures status of the department. In questioning the professionalism of management, Michael reflects a shared frustration with Connor. In an update some years later, Michael confirmed that the department had remained on special measures status and that this was leading to feelings of disaffection and low morale within the team.

> Being under the special measures in the department for myself and other lecturers has not been helpful, it's been a hindrance as we don't know when there will be some sort of re-evaluation of this, when these special measures will come to an end. It seems a bit like this has been going on now endlessly for years with no resolution.

Michael's experiences suggest a decline in the quality of media provision that could be linked to changes to the department's infrastructure. All three shared feelings of uncertainty reflecting an unstable FE environment. In Connor's case, this manifested in a lack of career progression and developmental enhancement, which provides insights into possible impacts from funding cuts on teaching staff and their development. David's feelings of uncertainty linked to his barriers in being able to develop long-term strategies for the college. David's position reflects the challenges that rapid policy change can present for college management in planning for the future in terms of funding, provision, and areas of focus. In Michael's case, feelings of uncertainty linked to a lack of job security and the future of the media department. Michael's concerns represent the ongoing pressure that creative FE departments can find themselves under in a policy framework that favours the sciences over the arts as represented in coalition educational policy under Michael Gove. Michael confirmed these fears over the course of the study, as he shared concerns over the future of media education.

> I'm not very hopeful with the current government and, in particular, dear Mr Michael Gove. There are lots of policies they seem to be trying to implement that I can't see benefitting in the long term. I hope this won't affect media education.

Michael's concerns relating to the quality of policy in long-term contexts and the future of media education echo broader literature that problematises the subject's identity and perceived lack of value in 14-plus curriculum contexts.

Staff perspectives on the effectiveness of South College differed significantly, representing a continued disconnect between management and lecturer perspectives and the absence of a shared vision and ethos. David positively summarised his experiences of managing South College and emphasised the positive trajectory the college was now on:

It's been a fabulous experience. It's the first time I've been a principal. I've not been a principal before. So you know I'm very lucky to have had the opportunity. It's been a hugely enriching experience in terms of learning how to do things, how not to do things. When you look at performance in this year we're significantly ahead of last year in terms of retention, we're not at national benchmarks for the sort of headline rates, we're at the average which is great in terms of where we were because we were significantly below the average. I expect that to continue, I expect that over the next three years the college should be in the position where it could be judged to be a good college with an ability to continue to improve and develop towards an outstanding college.

Michael shared negative experiences of management style during the period:

The first meeting with the faculty head [was] quite awkward and negative, he didn't seem to have much confidence in my abilities and would often go to my line manager rather than directly coming to me, which I felt was very unprofessional. Art had precedence over media and that there seemed to be some inferiority complex going on or something. It started to fail and now it's over stretched.

Michael's emphasis on a lack of professionalism among management and divisions between art and media represent a problematic management dynamic. Non-media specialist management positioning themselves as media experts in part spurred this on. As Michael recalls:

> There's a lot of difficulties there as well and with negative criticism in a teaching context. My current manager started giving me advice that I should do more practical work in my class and trying to tell me what animation I should do. Given in mind I'd specialised and studied animation you know, and this is someone who has no inclination about what that entails to deliver animation. This wasn't just me; other people were feeling the same thing, that this is someone trying to give advice when they're untrained in that area.

Michael's experiences indicate a continued undermining of management in respect to his performance and teaching. It appears that middle and upper management under David's crisis management was increasingly marginalising lecturer voices. This reflects a marginalised dynamic between lecturers and managers whereby lecturers like Connor and Michael felt unsupported, undermined, or ignored. Linking Michael's experiences to David's, the prevalent theme of disconnection between management perspectives and lecturer experience re-emerges. Michael's position within the department was uncertain because of his hourly paid teaching status. As he recalls, job uncertainty was a continued source of concern for him at the time.

> I felt a bit afraid I suppose that I would lose my job. It was a horrible time because lots of good lecturers left or were made redundant. I was in a really awkward position, because I wanted to make that transition to

full-time lecturer, and I'd prepared for this interview, I was ready in my suit waiting. Then told by my head of department that I'm afraid they had to cancel it and that the post might not be available, and it was a real error on their behalf. I think it was due to restructuring, there was some very flimsy excuse.

Michael's experiences reflect management cultures within the department that appear reactionary rather than strategic, and a breakdown in communication appears to compound divisions between management and lecturers within the department.

In contrast to Connor's views of management and their invisibility, David expressed a comparatively optimistic view, identifying positive shifts in communication styles in the college, because of new management approaches and restructures.

I would agree there's been consolidation because that was necessary and so there have been reductions in head count. That was necessary better financial control. I would like to think that culturally there's been a change in terms of people being more aware of the sector, of the way things happen and why they happen and being more prepared to be involved in that change. I think a lot of that's down to the transparency and communication, so people understand, they might not agree with what's happening [pause] and I don't expect everybody to agree with what's happening.

The disparity between these staff views is indicative of the disconnection between staff on the ground and leadership; this resonates with the broader FE discussion in Chapter 1.

Connor's summary of the various principals at the college, including David, testify to a perception that little has changed, but he also notes weak internal communication between the management and the managed. It is also ironic that David's sense of grievance at the lack of information and guidance from external policymakers exactly mirrors Connor's views on the state of internal communications under David's leadership. Despite the challenges expressed by David, he did share a positive outlook for the sector's future under the new coalition government.

> We will continue to be the sort of forgotten sector … very much overlooked. Although you know the coalition government at the moment have got a couple of fans of FE in the two main departments, so John Hayes has talked very positively about FE. And in fact, Nick Clegg, when he did one of his major speeches just after the election, he did that in an FE college – now I don't think that got noticed as much. I think it'll be interesting to see how it changes, there's a slightly different attitude and you get a sense [that] there are a couple of people in government in influential roles that are fans of FE …

Teacher training

The gift of hindsight enables us to conclude that David's optimism from 2011 would strongly contrast with the educational policy narrative that occurred thereafter under the coalition's Education Secretary, Michael Gove.

Initially a trainee teacher, Michael had secured some hourly paid classes within the media department to supplement his training.

Unusually, Michael had opted for an in-service PGCE without the securement of an existing teaching post or prior teaching experience. This placed Michael in a problematic position within the department, which was experiencing rapid and demanding change.

> It's easy for me to say that the PGCE experience was negative – but it mainly was except for my mentor who was also doing some level 2 teaching and was extremely supportive and was there to answer any questions. If it hadn't been for this, perhaps I would not have completed the PGCE, given up on teaching and it would just have been another qualification, tick a box done. But I was like, right! If I'm going to do it, it's going to be a career, that I'm going to put all my energy and efforts into.

Michael's experiences of a positive mentoring relationship in among a mostly negative training experience represent the value of a supportive mentoring relationship in post-compulsory teacher training contexts. He relates these experiences specifically to his early level 2 media teaching.

> I think it was just the way the PGCE was structured. It didn't seem to deal with those sort of BTEC learners that seem to be a different type of learner. It was a struggle for me. It wasn't a natural feeling to go into teaching. I had to really build myself up to step into the classroom. At one point there was quite a large level 2 cohort, some with quite different behavioural issues going on. For what the first few months I would sometimes

take that personally, if they were behaving in a certain inappropriate manner or if they were late and not attending classes. It took me a long time to understand that the meaning of teaching isn't to develop any sense of a style. Like many teachers I was learning and finding my way through that.

Michael's feelings of a lack in preparedness to teach level 2 resonates with studies conducted by Bathmaker and Avis (2007) into trainee teachers' experiences of low-level vocational teaching. However, I have to question Michael's rationale for doing an in-service PGCE without prior teaching experience. This point is especially prevalent as much of Michael's negative experiences concerning the PGCE connect to his lack of feeling prepared to carry out the teaching itself.

In between a problematic merger and restructuring of the media department, Michael did recall some positive experiences of reconnecting with his art background in some entry-level art teaching.

There was a short period of time where that seemed to work for me and I was fortunate enough that I got to do a bit more of the arts aspect. So painting or sculpture on a very small scale to entry-level learners, so it was an enjoyable time.

Michael's emphasis on returning to his original discipline reflects nuanced subject distinctions within the creative arts. Michael's transition into media teaching had been somewhat serendipitous following on from a support role. In reconnecting with his original discipline, Michael was able to enjoy the teaching process more than he had been thus far. It is possible to conclude that Michael's early negative experiences of teacher training and media facilitation can be linked to two key factors. Firstly, that he was on an in-service PGCE that is designed for lecturers in existing teaching posts and therefore lacked the experience required for an in-service training context. Secondly, that he was training to teach in a discipline that he had not trained in, and therefore had to learn the media subject alongside his teacher training within a "fragmented and unsupportive media department".

This aspect of Michael's narrative speaks to lecturer recruitment and pedagogic practices within South College and the media department. Had departmental standards and its media education ethos weakened in a state of flux? Was the absence of a media-specific manager negatively impacting the department's media education identity and credibility?

Considering Michael's overall experiences, it is possible to identify a notable shift in his views of level 2 learners. Whereas, in the previous quote, he classifies the level 2 learner as a particular "sort of BTEC student", implying a homogenous group of challenging students, in 2015 Michael reflects a nuanced awareness of the level 2 learner as he profiles his current cohort.

> This year for instance there's a real mix as we were talking about with behavioural issues etc., learning difficulties, but some very articulate students. You can see that it's just a confidence issue or something. One learner in particular really high grades ended up on level 1, erm, I assessed him quite early on and then we got him onto level 2. And he's now progressing but it's taken a

good term and a half just for him to get his confidence up, his confidence was absolutely shattered beyond belief, because of receiving such low grades and being predicted such higher grades.

Michael appears to have developed an astute understanding of the level 2 learner which in part can be attributed to an accumulation of experience and exposure to level 2 teaching, but also in part to his own lived experiences of being a level 2 learner.

All three staff appeared to struggle with the impacts of rapid policy change differently but with shared feelings of marginalisation in their roles, whether this manifested in leading South College during its difficult times through a turbulent policy landscape in David's case – or whether, as was the case for Connor and Michael, this meant a constant adjustment to their practice as defined by internal and external levers.

Moving towards stability?

David envisioned a strong and stable South College as he stepped out of his principal role in 2011. He emphasised the measures that had been put into place under his leadership, to ensure that the college move towards stability.

The structure, the approach, the attitude, and ethos of the governing body has changed significantly over the last year. Now we've got a group of governors who better reflect the need that the college has. Who are better placed to drive the college on and lead the college. The previous governing body was a hindrance to the college. I've worked very hard along with some others to reshape that group of people and help them understand their role better. So we've got a new clerk, who's done a fabulous job in terms of getting them to operate and function as a governing body should and that's a significant change that's happened. They take that role very seriously and they need to function well. And they weren't functioning well.

Using David's observations of formerly poor governance, the college governors can be considered as the key mediators. David's observations on the issues affecting South College represent a narrative that was far more complex than the Learning Skills Council-triggered problematic merger. His reflections represent a range of systemic problems, which connect to weak governance, a problematic college professional culture, and financial mismanagement.

It could be argued that, as David held the principalship on an interim basis, it was perhaps beyond his capacities to address the broader issues at South College. However, David did acknowledge the need for a healthy churn in management and wanted to encourage some of the college's long-serving managers to move on to other colleges. Perhaps if David continued in his role as principal at South College, some of the broader issues such as the lack of career progression opportunities for staff like Connor might have been addressed.

We've got some great people in the college. But we've still yet to get to the stage where we're starting to get them to churn and move on. I hope that we start to produce managers that move on to take up senior roles, principalships, vice principalships in other colleges in the sector so that you know in 10 to 12 years' time when you're meeting principals and senior managers they will be pleased to say that actually I was at South College as part of my development and you know South College is a place to go to in terms of being developed as a practitioner and a manager.

The role of FE

David's views on education indicated a clear distinction between the role of FE in comparison to other education sectors and leniency towards a business-orientated model that highlighted the importance of FE as a provider of good vocational education and apprenticeships. David's views are indicative of a pro-marketisation approach to FE that is in line with broader policy rhetoric.

In David and Michael's case, FE functioned as a second chance as both used FE to either retake level 2 after failing GCSEs or return to study. The sample followed vocational training routes in pursuit of their chosen fields and commented on their alignment with the ethos of FE, with its tradition of technical education. Paradoxically, although Connor prided himself on his academic abilities, he recalled a lack of engagement with the school style of teaching, an experience also shared by Michael. Their experiences suggest that FE has developed a different pedagogy to that of schools and it attracts people, both students and staff, who have not found it easy to connect to the ethos of school and often felt alienated by their experiences there.

Although staff shared the FE ethos of providing second chances, they all differ in their experiences of policy churn, and in their perspectives on policy and learning. The lack of connectivity between David and the two lecturers reflects a problematic and often messy mediation, which, based on Michael and Connor's experiences, is often lacking in information, rationale, and support. This is reflected in Michael's lack of clarity regarding departmental "special measures", and Connor's emphasis on ineffective leadership. It can be argued that the leadership ideologies from David that accompanied institutional change were not clear to Connor and Michael, and therefore potentially tricky to mediate in a climate of uncertainty. The oral histories presented here identify staff experiences like those of many FE learners. This may have been in the shape of failure at school as was the case for Connor, or through taking a break post-16 in pursuit of employment and re-entering education as a mature student, as was the case for David and Connor. Although staff differed in professional backgrounds and their positions within South, it is interesting to observe the overlapping ties between their lived experiences and the experience of the students they would have encountered in their teaching.

Funding and policy were identified as the most significant external levers by staff. In mapping staff's longitudinal experiences to these external levers, it was possible to identify direct and indirect effects on the South College's ecology. In David's view, the central focus of policy enactment was a cross-institutional drive to self-improvement and better financial self-management. The media department, which represented a microcosmic element of the college, could be seen to be experiencing the filter down as a rippling effect.

3

The experiences of negatively classified learners in their own words

Now it's time to meet the individual learners who took part in the study. We'll then focus on their school experiences, told in their own words, and consider whether the young people in this study were awarded the FE second chance they had been seeking.

Learning objective: Drawing on young people's experiences

- To enhance educators' awareness of the broader issues at play in the lives of young people so that institutional systems and learning structures and approaches can be assessed for effectiveness.

- To encourage educators to draw on the experiences of the young people in this study to develop nuanced understandings of learner contexts and complexities.

- To discourage educators from ascribing negative classifications to learners and, instead, to make holistic and deliberate choices in their support of learners at risk of being negatively classified.

Learner contexts

The young people who participated in the study were a diverse group; there was a mix of genders, races, socio-economic classes, and ages. However, they all shared a common experience of school failure and a classification of "low ability" that was given to them. They were also all enrolled as BTEC level 2 media students at South College at the point of joining the study.

Richard

Richard joined South College in 2004, aged 14, on the advice of his youth worker after being expelled from his secondary school. A severely dyslexic student, he joined a range of lower-level vocational courses in art and then media. Richard moved into a pure media provision in 2005 via the year 9 vocational equivalent Bridge to Foundation course, and then progressed onto the BTEC Introductory Diploma in 2006. He was offered an opportunity to complete level 2 embedded assessment alongside his level 1 peers, with a view towards direct entry onto the level 3 media course, but was unable to complete this. Instead, in 2007, he progressed onto the BTEC First Diploma, while many of his level 1 peers moved on to the level 3 National Diploma qualification. During this time, Richard was experiencing domestic and financial problems and was unable to regularly attend the course. Subsequently, Richard reached an agreement with the media department to suspend studies and return to the course the following year, allowing him time to resolve his personal circumstances.

In 2008, Richard re-enrolled on to the BTEC First Diploma media course. He found the course unchallenging, paper-heavy, and repetitious, partly because he had attempted the course twice before and was familiar with its content and assessment. When interviewed, Richard reflected negatively on teaching and learning on the course, and on his peers. Although Richard successfully passed this course and progressed onto the level 3, he was never officially notified of this outcome. Richard applied for the BTEC National Diploma audio strand, but this pathway was withdrawn on the first day of term without consultation with learners. During the study, Richard expressed disappointment at the way this was managed, and frustration at not being able to undertake the level 3 pathway of his choice.

Richard's financial difficulties persisted over the course of his later studies at South College, and these continued to affect his attendance. He underwent various disciplinary actions as a result, and although he would share his challenges with staff in disciplinary settings and receive staff assurances and agreed support plans, this did not reflect in departmental practice. Richard continued to be put through further disciplinaries relating to lack of attendance and became increasingly frustrated with this. Richard's time at South College ended in 2011 when he was withdrawn from the level 3 course while in his final year. At last contact, Richard had returned to live with a parent after a spell of homelessness and was unemployed, classifying as NEET (Not in Education, Employment or Training).

Rachel

Rachel initially attempted the BTEC First Diploma in media in 2006 and then again in 2009, this time successfully completing the course with a distinction. During the study, she shared her experiences of secondary school and the circumstances which brought her to South College. Her studies at South College were frequently interrupted due to financial constraints, due to which she was often engaged in low-skilled work. In addition, during her six years of study at South College, the institution faced some significant structural changes, the impacts of which reverberated across all departments, including the media department, in which Rachel was then a student. At interview, Rachel acknowledged these changes with reference to high staff turnover and a drop in quality across teaching, learning, and assessment, but with little awareness of broader institutional contexts.

Despite these challenges, she went on to successfully progress to the BTEC level 3 in media, achieving an overall triple distinction and securing a place at the university on an advertising degree. At last contact, Rachel explained that she did not complete this degree, instead choosing to take a year out of her studies in 2013, to work in retail. In 2014, she then transferred to a BA (Hons) in interior architecture and design at the same university that originally granted her a place on the advertising course and graduated in 2018. Rachel currently works as an admin assistant in a local painting and decorating company.

Kate

Kate joined the BTEC First Diploma media course at South College in 2006, after withdrawing from formal education for approximately two years. She lacked previous qualifications when she joined the college, but she went on to the BTEC National Diploma, after successfully completing the BTEC First Diploma. During the study, Kate recalled negative experiences of her secondary school, including detached teachers and peer bullying. These experiences led her to leave school, and she spent two years travelling with her family and taking part in professional film shoots, an activity made possible through her father's work in the industry.

Her time at the college totalled three years, during which she undertook BTEC media qualifications at levels 2 and 3, and when interviewed she recalled her time at the college positively. At the time of the main interview of the study, her BTEC National Diploma was ending, and Kate was preparing for study at a London university on a media and communications bachelor's degree. During her degree course, Kate fell pregnant and withdrew from her studies to concentrate on raising her child. At last contact, she was living as a single mum with no intention of returning to study in the near future.

Tyrone

Originally from Zimbabwe, Tyrone came to the UK in 2003 and attended a local secondary school from year 9. Tyrone's experiences of school were largely negative. He failed his GCSEs in 2006, after which he undertook a BTEC level 2 in leisure and tourism, and an AS-Level in media. He joined South College in 2008 as a BTEC level 2 media student. Already in possession of a pass at BTEC level 2 and a grade C in AS media, Tyrone found himself repeating BTEC level 2 due to the lack of places on the level 3 media course that he had originally applied for. At the point of enrolment, Tyrone was unaware of the duplication in qualification and, once aware, requested a transfer onto the level 3 course, but this was not accommodated. He went on to progress onto the BTEC level 3 and A2 media courses in 2009, after completing the level 2. Tyrone's time at the college ended in 2011 with successful completion of the BTEC National Diploma and A2 qualifications in media. He was able to secure a place at university on a bachelor's degree in telecommunications and networking. Tyrone graduated in 2015 and at last contact he confirmed that he was employed as a test analyst in a professional services company.

Abid

After negative experiences at school, and having failed his GCSEs, Abid joined South College as a BTEC level 2 ICT student in 2007 before moving onto the BTEC level 2 in media in 2008. Identifying as an "academic" style learner, his initial preference was for more theoretical content, and he would have preferred to follow a more traditional general qualification pathway on to A Levels, if his GCSEs had allowed this. The lack of progression opportunity from the BTEC First Diploma onto the A Level programme at South College also prevented him from pursuing A Levels after the level 2. Abid went on to progress to the BTEC level 3 in media, which he successfully completed in 2011, but he chose not to pursue higher education after leaving South College. At last contact, Abid was employed in his family's restaurant business.

Dominic

Dominic undertook the BTEC level 2 media course at South College in 2006, aged 16. He has been diagnosed with the little-known condition Angelman Syndrome, which manifests with symptoms recognisable in some specific learning difficulties (SpLDs). During the study, he recalled his lack of access to suitable special educational needs (SEN) support during his time at school and perceived this as being a contributory factor in not achieving his GCSEs. Dominic shared negative school experiences, including difficult relationships with his teachers and peers. He did not successfully complete the BTEC level 2 in media and left South College in 2007.

He went on to pursue a series of voluntary and low-skilled jobs and participated in an apprenticeship offered by hair salon chain Headmasters, which he did not successfully complete. In 2011, Dominic chose to re-attempt further education and enrolled onto a BTEC level 3 in animal management at a different FE college. He went on to progress onto a foundation degree in animal welfare and behaviour, followed by a BSc in the same subject at the same college, which he completed in 2016. Dominic currently works as a dog carer and driving assistant.

Learner lived experience

Having "met" the learners from a distance, let's consider how they describe their experiences – in their own words – and how these experiences might relate to the theoretical context that exists now and existed at the time of the study. What do these learners say about themselves, and does it match up with how policy and academic discourse understands them?

Negative school experiences

All learners described negative school experiences and FE second chances that resonated with broader literature of the time (see Bathmaker and Avis, 2007; Brown and Pollard, 2006; Coffield *et al.*, 2007; Collinson and Collinson, 2009; Hayward *et al.*, 2005).

Richard: I went to three schools and each and every single one of them was fucking useless, they were all shit. Like they literally had no idea what they were going on about. The worst school was a school that I went to the longest.

Rachel: The school I went to, it wasn't that great [laughs].

Kate: I went to *****, I left because I got bullied and stuff like that and then I didn't really go [to] secondary school.

Abid: Used to go to ***** Secondary School, at the time it really wasn't the best but I got through it, five years. I just thought like the learning process could have been like, so much more better.

Othering

Some prevalent themes that emerged from Richard, Tyrone, and Dominic's accounts were segregation in school based on SEN or behavioural issues:

Richard: I have quite serious dyslexia so instead of getting you some extra help or whatever they would just like fob it off as behavioural problems so you wouldn't actually go to real lessons, you just sit in this building which is full of behavioural problem students and you wouldn't do anything, you'd just sit there all day.

Tyrone: The [science] class I was in, there was a lot of unruly students like, you know, cussing at the teacher a lot of the time. So the teacher would often just let them do their thing and she would separate the ones that don't wanna do work and leave the ones that do wanna do work on one side.

Dominic: Because I was quite a problem student they sort of shoved me aside and I never really got any help at school.

Here, we see learner dissatisfaction fuelled by a process of othering. Individuals who are perceived as "challenging" on the premise of their behaviour or educational needs are segregated from the mainstream culture of the classroom. This readiness to segregate is in conflict with policy and academic rhetoric on the importance of inclusivity in teaching and learning in schooling and arguably contributes to the shaping of an individual's identity as a social outsider – as in the cases of Richard and Tyrone.

Lack of progression choices

Following on from this, Richard describes how his experience of exclusion, in the shape of segregated learning at school, led directly to a lack of subject choices for his progression.

Richard: I didn't have much choice cos I wasn't allowed to do textiles or engineering or food tech, so my choices were PE or history. And then they wonder why you have behavioural problems or why you start kicking off and it's like, well, it's just frustrating, isn't it, when you're just not being taught.

Poor teacher relationships

Richard's negative schooling experiences disconnected him from the central culture of the school and led him to intense feelings of disaffection and hostility towards his teachers.

Richard: Teachers at all the schools I went to weren't really teachers, they're just bullies, they're just paid bullies, that's all they are. There's no trust at all… they see you as numbers rather than people, if you know what I mean? You're just a student, you're just, you know, shut up, be quiet, sit at the back, you know, sit over there, be ignored.

Kate shared similar negative experiences of private school, with an emphasis on the lack of teacher acknowledgement of learners as individuals.

Kate: Well they were useful when you went the first day, but after that, they just sort of told you where to go and to sit down on the seat. They'd be like that's what they told you to do and basically that was it. I couldn't like generally talk to them because I didn't know them that well and they weren't very nice at all. And the head teacher wasn't very nice even though in her letters she sounded like a nice person but when you actually went she wasn't at all. And it seemed very fake as well so if they could try and not be fake that'd be wonderful.

Abid also recalled similar experiences, with specific reference to lack of support from teachers.

Abid: It was literally writing things down on the board, copying, and doing it yourself basically. So the extra help really wasn't there, because sometimes they wouldn't be specific in what they wanted and other times just maybe telling you to do this and you wouldn't be able to answer questions and it got a bit mixed up sometimes.

These learner experiences school cultures that fail to recognise learners as individuals and as creative agents. When Abid was asked for his opinions on how approaches in his school could have been improved, he responded by stating that teachers should try "to listen to the students and not treat them like children, so they get the best out of their education". He went on to note that he "learnt quite a lot, the classes I was in sometimes they were quite loud and quite disruptive, but I just got my head down and did my work, and that's about it".

Abid's emphasis on ignoring disruptive and loud classes reflected issues in classroom management at his school. His account of keeping his head down represents an element of academic self-motivation in spite of his school environment. In Abid's case, his school did not offer him a consistent opportunity to learn, and he was negotiating between directed and self-directed learning.

Disillusionment and escape

As we have seen, all students shared a perception of stratification in their school experiences. In all cases, this perception seemed to trigger a shift from learners seeing schooling as positive to disillusionment with the system. Richard and Rachel's shared experiences of disaffection at school, and their subsequent routing into 14-plus alternative provisions, is indicative of their search for an alternative to school.

Richard: After I got expelled from the last school, there was nowhere else I could go, I didn't have any GCSEs, anything like that. When I left school I had like not a lot of choices. The only reason I even knew that you could go to college when I got kicked out of school … if it wasn't for my youth worker telling me I could have gone to college then I'd probably wouldn't have gone to college until I was like 16, 17 … so I would have wasted all those years.

Rachel: I found out about coming to college one day a week, so yeah I decided to do that [because it] sort of like didn't exactly go right for me during the end of school.

Both learners identified the vocational link programme as a welcome opportunity to escape school. However, contrary to the 14-plus reform policy (DfES, 2002) rhetoric of the time, neither saw the programme to enrich and supplement their general education. Instead, the programme served different purposes for each learner. In Richard's case, 14-plus provisions offered a last chance after expulsion from his third school and were prompted by a conversation with his youth worker. In contrast, Rachel's experiences indicate the search for an alternative, facilitated by her mother's social network. In both cases, information regarding the provision appears to have been limited, suggesting a lack in guidance from their schools. Despite the different circumstances that brought Richard and Rachel onto the South College 14-plus, the programme represented a last chance to escape from a school system that they felt was failing them. Rachel recalled perceptions of 14-plus vocational link options being available for learners with behavioural issues.

Rachel: Well, basically, it [vocational link course] was mainly only available to people who had difficulty at school, like with behaviour. I weren't one of them people, but I got offered the chance because my mum found out through somebody else and, er, basically like bullied one of the women into letting me get onto it. [So I started at Year] 10, [for] just one day.

***

FE: Broader choice for all, or a dumping ground for the difficult?

There is a conflict between how learners perceive vocational link provision, based on their first-hand experience, and the broader discourse. Framing 14-plus provision as an option for difficult students risks undermining its status as a means of broadening choice for all learners in general education who seek to enrich their programmes of study by vocational components. Linking this to what Ball (1993) has to say about how some schools stratify learners perceived as challenging to appear data strong, it is likely that schools like Rachel's respond to "difficult" learners by using 14-plus provision as a means of segregation. If this is the case, it problematises the role of FE, repositioning the sector as a learning site for disaffected and disengaged learners who no longer have a place in the mainstream cultures of their schools.

Rachel's disaffection with education when at school, and her inclination towards more practical learning, identified her as the policy-typified low-ability vocational learner; however, her high GCSE grade predictions challenged such assumptions.

Changing minds, restricted options, and narrow focus

It was not Rachel's ability but her negative school experiences that prompted her to seek the alternative offered by the 14-plus vocational link programme. In 2005, she was enrolled on the health and social care provision at South College, due to an earlier interest in midwifery. However, her interests changed at least twice during this, indicating a caution against policies that promote early subject specialisation for young people. Through her experiences and perceptions, Rachel feels that steering young people too early into specialisms can restrict their future options.

Rachel: [At South College] I was on health and social care. Well the course turned out not to be what I thought it would be about and my priorities changed and instead I looked more into what I wanted to do and decided I [didn't want to do] the course I ended up being on, I wanted to do the audio and music course.

Similarly, Richard initially participated in lower-level art courses as part of his link provision, but then moved onto media.

Richard: They said I had to do media, I really thought it was going to be more like performing arts. I was like I really don't want to do that and then when I came here and I had such brilliant teachers and I found out what it was and like I've always been interested in films, especially animation, so it was brilliant, which is why, after art, I came on full-time as a media student. Then I started the media course.

Had these learners continued with their original choices, they would have been restricted to that option as they progressed through qualification levels. Their initial interests in health and social care and art changed once they had engaged with the subjects at South College. In effect, the college allowed these learners an opportunity to trial the discipline before committing to a specialism. As a result, they were still able to consider different vocational subjects at 16 and pursue media at levels 2 and 3.

In contrast to the experiences of most learners who had pursued level 2 media because they had failed their GCSEs, Kate had not got as far as having attempted her GCSEs. Being out of mainstream education for two years before enrolling at South College, Kate was initially considered for the level 1 BTEC Introductory Diploma in media. However, her bank of qualifications, obtained via distance learning offered by a United States university, allowed her to be considered for the level 2 course instead. The only participant to have initially attended an independent school,

Kate's experiences of schooling nonetheless echoed those of the rest of the young people.

Kate: It was very structured, like you couldn't really move around. They'd be like, you're going to C. Independent School and then normally most people came before they were already in the primary schools, probably knew each other so it was like quite a close community. They were like you go from here and you can go on to university and that's how you will be, you can't do anything else because it is just education failed.

Kate's comments on her school's narrow focus on university as the only successful destination sit uncomfortably with some educational policy rhetoric that stresses the need for more expansive progression routes. Institutional attitudes such as those expressed by Kate's school are indicative that parity of esteem between the "academic" and "vocational" routes remains an uneasy dynamic within some schooling cultures.

Failure shapes identity

Learners drew causal connections between their negative experiences and the quality of support and teaching and learning at their schools. They also shared perceptions of poor classroom management – with a particular lack of support for those with SEN or behavioural issues – as barriers to their learning.

The culture of stratification reflected in these learner narratives thus far is indicative of systemic stratification on micro and macro levels. These learners all felt excluded from and disaffected by their schools. However, the reasons varied. In some instances, their schools literally segregated learners deemed difficult from the mainstream culture of the school, and subsequently from general education and the option of achieving their GCSEs. In other cases, like in Kate's school, a social division between vocational and academic progression was created.

All learners reflected on their experience of failure at school in both a literal and a metaphorical sense. This can be defined in their distinctions of objective and subjective "failure", where school grades signify the objective, and their sense of failure and perceived low academic ability signify the subjective. We can see here how school failures can shape learners' academic identities (Higham and Yeomans, 2006) as they navigate their schooling and begin to enter into FE.

Objective experiences of failure

In Kate's case, she struggled to complete formal schooling because of bullying at school, and subsequently engaged with distance and informal modes of learning before enrolling at South College.

Kate: There was a whole palaver about when I did get bullied they lied and said I didn't. I went to Spain and Texas for two years and I came back and then got into South College. So [laughs] I didn't really have an education. When I wasn't at school I kept like studying stuff. I did like, like adult learning sort of like erm from home [through] Texas University. [That] year, I learnt all about the politics and stuff like that but then I left so I didn't finish the exam so …

In Richard's case, school expulsion led him to alternative provision at South College.

Richard: After I got expelled from the last school, er, there was nowhere else I could go, I didn't have any GCSEs, anything like that.

In both these cases, the learners were unable to complete their schooling and undertake their GCSEs. This is in contrast to the remaining young people, whose failure at school is represented by their poor GCSE grades.

Subjective experiences of failure

In terms of a more subjective idea of failure, we consider the learners' self-reflection, their own sense of failure, and the perceptions of their academic ability (both from themselves and from those around them). Most of these young people attributed their GCSE failure to many causes.

Rachel: They [GCSE grades] were all awful, I got predicted good grades, it's just when it came to they were all fails … I was disappointed in myself but I knew I weren't gonna do it … I am not good in an exam situation.

Abid: My exam results could have been better but overall I can't really complain, I was quite happy with what I had got. I wish that I had tried harder in maths to improve my grade because I really was not happy with it.

Dominic: GCSE-wise I didn't do amazingly well. I have learning difficulties as well which, so I can't like, I am not very good at handwriting, I can't write for long periods of time, er, my handwriting is atrocious [laughs], and learn things very slowly. I find it really hard concentrating for more than 20 seconds and short-term memory loss, always forgot what I was learning. Erm yeah, so didn't do amazingly well with those sort of things.

Tyrone remembered studying for exams and feeling initially confident that he would do well, but ended up not achieving the GCSE result he hoped for, in spite of long periods of revision. From these experiences, Tyrone concluded that he needed to redouble his academic efforts.

Tyrone: Cos the thing is I would go home, make sure I'd get all my books, revised and revised and revised, go in the exam, I'd do the exam, come out confident. I could've done better. I mean I knew I could've better myself so that's when I kinda told myself that I need to be on point all the time, I need to step my game up.

Dominic justified his results concerning his SEN while also acknowledging his problematic school persona because of behavioural issues. Tyrone and Abid share a commonality in their responses, with both concluding that they should have worked harder on their GCSEs, although Tyrone's account of lengthy revision periods and confidence in exam performance conflict with his emphasis on needing to work harder. Somewhat similarly, Rachel said she was "disappointed in herself", suggesting that she blamed herself. Except for Rachel, the remaining learners indirectly blamed their institutions for their failure.

***

How a sense of failure can evolve

Rachel's view of herself as a learner had developed from her reflections on her GCSE failure – the subjective drew from the objective, here. Her explanation for her failure included insufficient support from her parents: "It's my parents' fault because they went away on holiday during the exams, so I partied and fell asleep in some of my exams". But she also recognised that she did not manage exam assessment well, "I am not good in an exam situation", and was not ready to take full responsibility for her studies: "I didn't get the grades that I wanted at GCSE … [because of] I don't know, my behaviour I suppose in secondary school, my immaturity".

It is evident from Rachel's account how her sense of failure evolved over time, as she moved from this position of blaming others to some realisation of her own part in the outcome, arising from a process of self-reflection: "I didn't pay attention at school, I didn't think it was important, I never went. I suppose like if I could go back, like I wish like I'd actually paid attention". In this later disclosure, Rachel acknowledged responsibility for school truancy and disengagement and identified these behaviours as reasons for her failure. In hindsight, she regretted past behaviours and viewed these as having prevented her from progressing through a smooth and linear academic trajectory: "I wish like I'd actually paid attention because then I wouldn't be in the situation I am in now where I am 19 and still doing a GCSE-level course". Rachel went on to reflect on what she would do differently if she had her time again: "If I could go back, I would have done better, I would have paid attention. By now I should have been at uni, wasted too much time [laughs]".

Rachel's story, more than anyone else's, is ultimately one of success. However, she was not able to celebrate this fully, because of her underlying regret about failing her GCSEs and the subsequent time she spent trying to regain momentum towards higher-level study.

***

Identity is shaped by both objective and subjective failure

The accounts of all young people contained themes of blame, regret, and disaffection. Learners' self-identities were tied closely to their experiences at school and of GCSE failure. The relationship between negative feelings of school and GCSE outcomes was a persistent motif among the learners, and Kate's and Richard's cases were perhaps the most extreme – as they disconnected from the school system before undertaking their GCSEs. However, there are still distinctions between these two extreme cases.

The role of choice

Kate's situation arose from choice: she had family support for her decision to leave her independent school. In contrast, Richard's experiences tell the story of a system that has given up on him. His account describes increasing levels of disaffection. First, Richard speaks of his frustrations with his secondary school's policy of segregating "difficult" students and of his being branded as a problem because of his SEN. This later leads to anger when he is not permitted to select the GCSEs of his choice. The culmination of this process is Richard's expulsion, which confirmed his belief that the school was persecuting him. He felt justified in his disengagement, and in his subsequent disaffection with the school system, concerning the lack of learning opportunities that the school system offered him, arising from their view of him as a "difficult" learner. Richard continued adopting disaffected personas throughout the longitudinal interviewing process, frequently expressing entrenched frustrations with the education system. In Richard's case, this pattern of failure and of being failed, which formed through his schooling, was replicated in his later FE career.

Abid's accounts of schooling highlighted a lack of consistent support from teachers and the lack of clarity in teaching and learning. His account painted a picture of inconsistency and disorganisation, which impacted both his available choices and his sense of failure.

Abid: Sometimes they wouldn't be specific in what they wanted and other times they were just telling you to do this and you wouldn't be able to answer questions and it got a bit mixed up sometimes.

SEN, behaviour, and classroom management

The themes of a lack of school support for learners with SEN, and subsequent failure at school, were prevalent themes in both Dominic's and Richard's stories – in this case, it was the lack of support for their specific needs which they felt impacted their available choices and their experiences of failure. In both cases, their schools segregated them from the mainstream culture of the class, and this seems to have incubated a sense of failure and led to the formations of learning identities which contributed to their difficulties. In both cases, the learners reflected on their SEN and the challenges arising from their conditions as well as the lack of SEN support from their schools in assisting them through their general education. Moreover, in both cases, the link is identified between SEN and behavioural issues.

Richard: I have quite serious dyslexia so, um, instead of getting you some extra help or whatever they would just like fob it off as behavioural problems.

Dominic: I didn't like being told what to do and, er, I have learning difficulties as well, because I was quite a problem student they sort of shoved me aside and I never really got any help at school.

It seems that in both cases, being identified with a special educational need led to marginalisation rather than enhanced support. Richard's and Dominic's accounts tallied with Tyrone's experiences of schooling, where being identified as having a "problem" and being seen as "disruptive" led to being segregated in classrooms: "So the teacher would often just let them do their thing, and she would separate the ones that don't wanna do work". This strategy, while it might work at some level for the teacher, increases the marginalisation of the special needs learner: "I can't work in an environment where it's separated … cos if someone's making noise and someone is trying to work, it's not gonna work, I can't work in a noisy place".

Abid's earlier account of disruptive classes mirrored Tyrone's experiences of some classes at school being disruptive and poorly managed. Both learners acknowledged the challenges of studying in these environments.

Richard and Dominic's accounts also tallied with Tyrone's experiences of "problem" and "disruptive" students being segregated in classrooms, except, in their case, they would have been identified as the "problem students" and the potential cause of disruptions instead of SEN being the reason for segregation. As Tyrone's account demonstrates, teachers would ignore such learners, who were perceived as difficult and disengaged.

Tyrone: So the teacher would often just let them do their thing and she would separate the ones that don't wanna do work.

In Tyrone's view such classroom strategies compounded the problem of a disruptive classroom: "I can't work in an environment where it's separated … cos if someone's making noise and someone is trying to work, it's not gonna work, I can't work in a noisy place".

Rachel and Richard expressed similar views about how school practices exacerbated behavioural issues. Richard, for example, explained his behavioural problems as arising from his frustration at being segregated while Rachel recognised, in retrospect, that she was enacting a self-fulfilling prophecy:

Rachel: And I suppose that's why in ways you act up at school because you are trying to like I suppose live up to what they expect sort of thing.

Dominic also commented on school expectations and framed these as the context of his own experiences.

Dominic: I'd say secondary school was, I don't know if it's the same with all secondary schools but for me it was very sort of based on how well you did at school was based on how sort of popular you were with the teachers. If you were popular like with one teacher you were going to get sort of sorted in every class you were in and er yeah, people who were naughty just did not get any help and yeah, it was sort of based entirely on relationships with teachers.

In Richard's and Dominic's stories, their behavioural issues reflected a cycle of frustration for both learners who felt unsupported for their SEN and dismissed by the system.

These reflections by Tyrone, Richard, and Dominic on the lack of specialist support and the segregationist approaches of their schools problematise the reality of inclusive approaches to teaching and learning. The accounts also identify widespread practices which define the individual based on limited characteristics, such as an assumed ability based on SEN criteria or behaviour. However, some of the young people shared some positive experiences of individual schoolteachers who helped them navigate a challenging school environment.

Finding an ally

Dominic: Apart from one teacher who was my science teacher and he was also my form tutor. So he was with me throughout like the whole of my secondary school and erm, yeah he was really helpful. He got me through quite a lot of things and helped me out if I was in trouble and stuff like that, he helped me learn, so yeah. He was pretty good.

Tyrone linked his positive experiences to his English teacher who made the subject more accessible for him as he struggled to engage well with the subject.

Tyrone: The only good thing about English was the teacher. She kind of knew how to make everything easier. English just wasn't my thing cos, I mean when it came to poems and all that, I didn't quite understand English cos I didn't see the point of poems.

Rachel explained her positive experiences of some teachers concerning emotional support rather than teaching and learning.

Rachel: The school itself wasn't actually that great but I learnt lots of lessons from like some of the good teachers and from pupils and stuff. I'm quite a quick learner [so school equipped me with skills] yeah, it did. [The teachers were helpful], but not in [an] education way. If that makes sense? More like a personal way, like emotional way, yeah. [Laughs]

However, in all these cases, these singular experiences did not reshape their overall negative perceptions of their schools.

GCSEs

In all cases where GCSEs were undertaken and failed, learners appeared to have undertaken a different suite of GCSEs. In Rachel's case, she recalled finding out that her GCSE in expressive arts was not recognised as a valid qualification by colleges. This confirms Wolf's (2011) findings of students being "steered" (2011, p. 83) into valueless qualifications.

Tyrone: In GCSE I took business studies, I liked it but was a bit too hard. Media studies. I took um, science was compulsory, maths was compulsory, English. Then I took um, DT, I forgot the exact word for it but it's like woodwork.

Rachel: I did the core ones [GCSEs], er maths, English, science and RE but I didn't do RE, I did expressive arts, which isn't a recognised GCSE I found out. I did, er, food technology, I did geography but then dropped it – and then health and social care, oh and IT.

In Rachel's case, her GCSEs supplemented her vocational link arrangement with South College on the health and social care provision. However, her inclusion of health and social care when recounting her GCSE options is reflective of her lack of awareness of vocational link levels and their nature. This provision was in fact not the equivalent to GCSE but was closer to year 9 or vocational link entry-level provision. Rachel's experience was indicative of a lack of wider information about post-school options, and mirrored the experiences of her fellow learners, who all had limited guidance and advice when transitioning into college. For example, Abid negatively recalled the lack of guidance available to him from school and his brush with the Connexions service.

Lack of progression guidance

Abid: After leaving school I wasn't really sure about what I was going to do next, where I was going to go and things like that. There was a Connexions office in my school but like they really were of no help whatsoever.

Dominic recalled a meeting with a career guidance counsellor: "when I was at school I remember I had a careers guidance counsellor come in, and he reckoned that I should have been a carpenter". He went on to share his surprise at the suggestion and was unclear on how the counsellor has concluded this … "and I have no idea how that linked at all but yeah. Er, I didn't, I decided not to go down that career path". Dominic's encounter with the career counsellor is indicative of an institutional emphasis on skill-based career options for "difficult" students. Comparatively, Kate, Rachel, and Richard had accessed information informally. In Kate's case, she was informed and assisted by a friend who was already enrolled onto a course at South College.

Kate: I heard it from a friend actually, she was like, she went every Friday for GCSEs, and she was like, oh it's [South College is] really good. And erm, I just generally rang them up and was like can I apply? And that was how

I did it.

Rachel had become aware of the college through her mother's network and was already cognisant of South College through the vocational link programme.

Rachel: The only thing I learnt about was the, it's IFP [vocational link course] isn't it? Yeah, that's the only thing that my mum heard that from someone else, they [the school] weren't that open about it. I just thought, because I was already at South College … I felt comfortable here, so I thought I'd come here and learn.

Richard, on the other hand, discovered some of the options available to him through his youth worker. He recalled that, had he not been told about the 14-plus South College option at the time, he would have been ignorant of the choices available to him, and out of education for two years until age 16. When reflecting on his experience of GCSEs (or lack thereof), Richard stressed the absence of information available from his school regarding vocational options available to him through college.

Richard: The school never told you anything like that, so … but South College took me. So, I came here instead of doing GCSEs.

Richard undertook a series of vocational courses during his time at South College aged 14–16, most of which he believed constituted GCSE equivalence.

Richard: For the first few years, I did art and design and IT and various other stuff. Art and design up to NVQ level 2 and everything else I think was GCSE level or below.

So that was all good.

Richard's perceptions of the courses that he was undertaking were different from the reality of the programme that South College had put together for him. Art and design were not offered as an NVQ (National Vocational Qualification) at the college, and the courses that he undertook in art and IT among others were at "taster" level and were not accredited courses. In Richard's case, he was being retained within the framework of mainstream education at any cost to prevent his disengagement from education, training, or employment. However, his lack of knowledge regarding the provision that he was on at South College as well as the lack of value of these qualifications problematises the role of pure 14–16 vocational provisions. Richard's experiences partially mirrored Rachel's situation at school, whereby she had taken a "GCSE" in expressive arts, only to discover later that the subject did not count as a valid GCSE by colleges. This further demonstrates the lack of information that was available to her while at school.

Vocational training prior to the study

Richard, Tyrone, and Abid all undertook vocational training before the First Diploma in media in various forms. Richard took unaccredited courses in art and IT, while Tyrone studied for the BTEC First Diploma in leisure and tourism and Abid enrolled in a BTEC First Diploma ICT programme at South College. All learners recounted different experiences of teaching and learning in these programmes. Only Richard had positive experiences with these vocational training programmes: "I had really good teachers, they seem to be a lot more helpful … in college". Tyrone and Abid were critical of their courses.

In Tyrone's case, he recalled the course as computer-heavy, though he found the customer service elements of the course enjoyable.

Tyrone: The leisure and tourism, there was no practical at all. It was just computers, computers, typing up loads of stuff and all, like throughout the whole year – [but] I like[d] the customer service part of it.

Tyrone's situation differed from the rest of the young people in that he continued at sixth form after his failure at GCSEs and was placed on a BTEC First Diploma, in leisure and tourism. His position on the First Diploma resulted from a lack of available vocational options and was indicative of the school selecting this programme of study for him.

Tyrone: I'd have loved to go straight onto AS instead of doing travel and tourism but, well, I kinda had to do it. It was kind of one choice cos they didn't have anything else besides travel and tourism in order to get the GCSEs I needed. I needed to do a subject like that [BTEC First] cos it was the equivalent of four GCSEs.

Tyrone's experience of joining the BTEC First Diploma in leisure and tourism mirrored Abid's account of enrolling onto the BTEC First Diploma in ICT: "it was the only course available at the time, so not really what I wanted to do". Both learners opted for these courses as they were the only ones available to provide the needed GCSE equivalence. Tyrone's situation was unusual in that he was also able to undertake an AS in media alongside the level 2 in leisure and tourism. He recalled the difficulties he experienced in securing a place on the AS at the time:

Tyrone: Then last year I then went on to do, um, cos I couldn't quite go straight onto AS cos I didn't get enough GCSEs cos I needed five of them. So I did a First Diploma in travel and tourism – my previous teacher insisted that I do AS [media] cos she said, well, I was good at it in the previous year so insisted I do, carry on with it, then she talked to the head of sixth form and they let me do it.

Tyrone was the only participant to have undertaken level 3 qualifications before joining South College. Tyrone successfully passed both the BTEC First Diploma with a "pass" and achieved a Grade C in the AS media. Tyrone's performance on the AS, in comparison to the BTEC First Diploma, represents a disjuncture between his actual and perceived academic abilities. Tyrone's assessment outcomes were better for the AS media than the BTEC First in leisure and tourism, but he concluded that he was better suited to practical rather than general academic-style learning. Situating Tyrone's experiences of the lack of practical learning on the BTEC First Diploma in leisure and tourism in the context of his choice to apply to South College for a more practical course proves paradoxical, as he had no prior experience of BTECs before this. Furthermore, this reflects Tyrone's emerging learning identity as a "practical learner" as shaped by his school classifications once he had failed his GCSEs.

Tyrone: I wanted something more practical-based so I checked out the courses here at South College because I had enough qualifications to go into a two-year course, so I applied here for a National Diploma course so I can do those two years instead of staying on there [*****] for two years doing the AS and the A2. So I applied here [as] I didn't wanna stay at ***** cos it was boring. I wanted to go to a different place.

However, it appears that Tyrone was able to conclude that his local FE college would be able to facilitate better practical vocational learning than his school could. His choice to leave parallels Richard and Rachel's pursuit of an alternative to school.

In addition to the influence on Tyrone's self-perception from his school, it is possible that he reached this conclusion about his "practical" learning identity because of his engagement with the coursework component of the AS media, which he much enjoyed.

Tyrone: I did AS media which also was very good, although it was more on the paperwork side but then there was a practical bit where I made a trailer of my own movie that I designed and that was good actually. I quite enjoyed it.

Abid's experiences of the ICT course were negative, and he recalled the course as being disorganised and not meeting his expectations.

Abid: I thought I would be learning like different aspects of computing and various other things, but it really wasn't like what I expected. Basically it was all, it was all a bit mixed up, a bit confusing at times because I didn't understand what was expected of me so I went to, er, my ICT lessons and they weren't really specific in what they needed from me so I found it quite like a daunting experience to be honest.

[…]

Basically, it was just being given all these applications to do, like, er, what was there, there were spreadsheet [sic], documents, I didn't really learn much about ICT, I was just learning about the applications and software.

However, this did not prevent him from reapplying for a low-level vocational course at South College after his efforts in ICT proved unsuccessful.

✳✳✳

Abid's attainment of a grade C in GCSE English, alongside his suite of GCSEs that enabled him to undertake a BTEC level 2 over a BTEC level 1, evidenced his academic abilities. This was reinforced in Abid's self-identification as an academic-style learner: "I am not that hands-on" and his later admittance, that grades allowing, he would have pursued a general academic programme of study such as A Levels. Again, here a theme of lack of choice is raised: the lack of provision for GCSE retakes prevented these young people from selecting the type of learning that they wanted to undertake, instead routing them into the low-level vocational provision and classifying them as vocational learners. In Dominic's case, there was a lack of clarity and support on next steps after failing his GCSEs: "yeah, so I had to sort of do that completely on my own, just sort of put together what I enjoyed doing and what I liked".

Students' lack of access to information and guidance is perhaps most vividly captured in Tyrone's account. Despite having undertaken and passed his First Diploma in leisure and tourism at school, he was unaware of the qualification's levels, which influenced his choices and access at South College and caused him a setback in the shape of retaking the level 2.

Tyrone: I wasn't aware of the difference between the First Diploma and the National Diploma. It wasn't made clear to me really so the way I saw it was it's just the same thing except that it's just the First Diploma was the start of the National Diploma.

Furthermore, all young people shared aspirations that reflected an uncomplicated general education pathway. Wolf's (2011) reference to the lack of central guidance outside of A Levels is collaborated in these accounts; learners initially attempted to re-enter mainstream education by undertaking level 2, and shared aspirations for progression onto level 3 courses and, in some cases, higher education, or career pathways. The young people's simplification of their post-failure trajectories and the role of their local FE college in supporting and facilitating these possibilities were key factors in establishing the learners' "learning identities".

In the theme of insufficient guidance and support, all learners were unaware that South College did not accept the BTEC First Diploma for entry into A Levels. Rachel later learnt this while on the BTEC National Diploma and queried the equivalence of BTECs to general education in this context.

Rachel: I don't get that because they expect a uni to accept it. I need to sort that out [laughs].

To an extent, the learning identities of these young people depended on how they felt they were classified at school; for example, their definitions of problem behaviour and of being perceived as having a low academic ability. In all cases, this helped form identification of learning styles. In some cases, learners identified themselves as practical students and unresponsive to general academic education. This was reflected in learners opting for vocational programmes post GCSE failure.

Journey to South College – summarising themes

We can see some common themes in the learners' experiences that led them to South College.

Lack of information and guidance

The lack of guidance and choice was a recurring theme for all learners, concerning programmes offered by their schools or South College. In all cases, learners had insufficient information relating to qualification levels. This supports findings from Wolf's (2011) work, which asserted a lack of adequate guidance and support available to students and concluded that, outside of A Levels, there was very little information for young people on vocational programmes.

> This has been done quite comprehensively in the past for the 14–16 age group, although, as we have seen, in recent years there has been an unexpected

and dramatic increase in the number of "vocational" awards offered to this age group. 16–19 education is very different. Outside A levels, it has operated with very little central guidance, let alone requirements that address the overall structure of students' programmes.

(2011, p. 105)

Learners' encounters with South College, then, appeared to be serendipitous, or even somewhat haphazard. In their pursuit of either an alternative to school or GCSE equivalence, learners enrolled on courses without sufficient knowledge of their currency towards their envisaged future trajectories. In Tyrone's case, this manifested as a retake of a qualification level that he had already passed, whereas in Richard's case, he continued to bank unaccredited qualifications under the impression that he was progressing through school-equivalent qualifications.

Insufficient knowledge of vocational courses affects trajectories

The lack of knowledge shared by these young people affected their choices and, in some cases, like Abid's, led to a "false start", as Abid's undertaking of a BTEC First Diploma in ICT later brought him no value. In all cases, the responsibility for the lack of guidance and information sits with their schools and South College; instances by all learners suggest that the institutions were driven by recruitment and attainment data rather than by the interests of these individuals.

There is a clear link between literature that criticises an oversaturation of 14–16 vocational provisions and its potential lack of currency and, hence, long-term value to learners. We see young people who, in their haste to reset their mainstream academic trajectories or escape the confines of schooling cultures, found themselves on low-level qualifications. In Richard's case, this manifested in unaccredited courses, while for Abid and Tyrone, it led to a lack of learning opportunities.

We can see that these young people joined their sense of academic self to their failure at school and subsequent pursuit of vocational options in FE. South College provided these learners with a choice of re-entering education when these learners felt that they were failing. In this context, the nature of their initial course choices becomes somewhat irrelevant, as the college offered them a way out of schooling when they most wanted this.

Conceptualising learner narratives of failure

Learner's narratives suggest complex and often messy trajectories into South College. All young people position the institution as an escape route out of secondary school. Experiences of failure feature strongly in their stories, which represent their status as school outsiders as much as their critical failure at GCSE. Experiences of negative schooling cultures appear to compound learners' feelings of otherness and self-identity as "outsiders", excluded from the system. The learners represent the atypical FE learner in their secondary school failures and consequent search for a second chance in FE. In summary, learner narratives represent a complexed and nuanced ecology at play, which often exceeds their exposures to learning and policy mediation. Their stories represent the long-term effects of learning experiences and exposures on young people and impacts on the formation of their self-identities and views of the world. Their shift onto level 2 media was serendipitous and followed messy trajectories through complex information and guidance frameworks. Learners shared different feelings of otherness within the general education framework; this was accounted for by the unique ecologies of their secondary schools, which, although different, shared commonalities in exclusionary practices. Learners' narratives resonated with the personal experiences of staff such as Michael, in the shape of their unsuccessful school outcomes and seeking a second chance in FE.

New beginnings?

Most young people shared experiences of "messy trajectories" before embarking on the level 2 media course. The learners began their journey into FE and South College at various points aged 14 to 16.

In the case of Richard and Rachel, their journey had begun much sooner, in the shape of South College's 14-plus low-level vocational provision (an outcome from newly released 14–19 policy). Both learners' journeys into level 2 were fragmented and serendipitous as they attempted a range of low-level courses and disciplines before moving into media.

Learners' motivations for studying media were also serendipitous to varying degrees as, except for Tyrone and Kate, learners had demonstrated limited knowledge and understanding of what studying lower-level vocational media would entail.

This resonates with research into media education offered by Buckingham (2017), who draws similar conclusions concerning learners' motivations for studying low-level vocational media. In all cases, learners made a conscious decision to opt for a vocational course. This links to their initial academic self-concepts whereby most of these learners self-identified as *practical*.

Rachel's journey into media was somewhat unusual. In the absence of places on her initially applied for music course, she had made a spontaneous decision on enrolment day to opt for media. She was able to secure a place on the level 2 media through a reference from a former vocational link college tutor and proceed onto a course she knew very little about. Rachel's experiences suggest that the college's enrolment infrastructure was weak and non-selective in its student recruitment processes.

Rachel: I chose to do the National Diploma in audio and music as I enjoy music. When I came to my interview and got told there was no place for any of the courses. I found out about media on enrolment day. It weren't exactly what I wanted to do but it was linked to music. So I begged my way onto it and got onto the course through reference. I was glad I chose it but I didn't really choose it.

Tyrone's experiences were problematic, as his original application for the National Diploma media course had been steered into level 2 media at interview. Already in possession of a level 2 qualification, Tyrone had been guided into repeating the level. Tyrone's experiences strengthen conclusions of inefficient student recruitment infrastructure.

Tyrone: I wanted something more practical-based so I checked out the courses here at South College because I had enough qualifications to go into a two-year course so I applied here for a National Diploma media course. I applied here, got given an interview, then I was told I haven't got enough qualifications to do a National Diploma. She told me it was practical-based too and I wasn't aware of the difference between the First Diploma and the National Diploma. It wasn't made clear to me really so the way I saw it was it's just the same thing. Whereas now I understand I had enough qualifications cos I'd already done a First Diploma.

Rachel and Tyrone's experiences of applying to South College reflect College principal David's accounts of the issues that interim management encountered regarding student recruitment data.

David: When we came here, you know we have a weekly senior management team meeting and asked for numbers of applications. It was very difficult to get the information in a format on a weekly basis that told us what we needed to know. We had a long list of courses and it didn't say well actually these students are 16 to 18, these are 19 pluses and these have applied, these have been interviewed, these have been enrolled, these have been rejected. We just didn't have that information available, so we had to get that information drawn out the system so we were clear and aware of where we were with applications. Because it's essential that on a regular basis we know. So it's things like that that frustrate and delay.

David's reflections on the broader issues affecting the college suggest a causal relationship between the college's weak data systems and recruitment and enrolment practices. Moreover, it is possible to conclude that the college's enrolment teams held limited knowledge of subject disciplines within the college. This is particularly prevalent in Rachel and Kate's accounts.

Kate: I heard it from a friend actually, she went every Friday for GCSEs and she was like, South College is really good. I just generally rang them up and was like, can I apply? And that was how I did it.

In Kate's case, an informal peer referral and a telephone conversation appear to have triggered her place onto media. Placing this in the context of her recent lack of qualifications, it is possible to conclude that low-level vocational media recruitment at the college was non-selective.

However, David observes the contradictions to this: "We're all chasing after the same students because we have targets to meet and, importantly, I have people who I have to keep in employment. So, if we don't hit our recruitment targets, then I have to make people redundant." This dynamic represents the tensions between the different layers of the South College ecosystem.

Richard's transition onto level 2 media was comparatively more straightforward but, like Rachel, he also expressed limited prior knowledge of the discipline. His reference to being "told" to do media implicates a steering process. Richard's experiences also indicate student recruitment dynamics, whereby creative subjects are perceived as interchangeable. Initially an art student, his steering into media suggests a lack of differentiation between the two disciplines. Learners' experiences thus far indicate that South College processes were ill equipped to advise and guide students transitioning into low-level vocational media courses. Furthermore, learners' lack of information on what vocational media would entail represents a limited college-wide understanding of media education. In comparison to the rest of the learners, Dominic's motivations to study media were fuelled by assumptions of what the course would entail. His passion for films had steered him to the level 2 media, though, as he admits, his level 2 exposures led him to move away from the subject.

Dominic: I wasn't entirely sure what I wanted to do. The reason I chose media at the time I was sort of just watching movies non-stop and over and over again. I'm still very interested in movies and I consider myself a bit of a rubbish critic moaning about films – but yeah for a career, I see what Rachel does and that's not my sort of thing.

Abid also shared limited knowledge of media at the point of application, but in contrast to the rest of the learners he expressed a strong motivation to use level 2 media as a progression lever for level 3. Dominic's and Abid's experiences echo broader media education discourse, which asserts that the discipline is often misunderstood or perceived as an easy option. In Abid's case, level 2 media was the last resort.

Abid: I couldn't get onto any other course and I thought to myself, hang on a second, I've tried everything else, nothing else is working and media seems like the right option. I just thought it was only a stepping-stone that I needed to get up to the next course. I'm kind of glad that I went on a First Diploma, so I could get loads of things underneath my belt, like, so I would be well equipped going into the National Diploma. I'd rather not go into the National Diploma without the First Diploma under my belt as I wouldn't have a grasp of what was going on. I don't think it's possible for me to actually finish FD then go into the world of work when I haven't even learnt anything.

Unique to the other learners, Abid demonstrates a clear vision of how level 2 can serve him academically and emphasises the qualification's lack of industrial value. Abid's perceptions of level 2 reinforce David's views that "level 2s serve the purpose of meeting the needs of students who didn't do as well as they'd hoped at school. A stepping-stone into where they wanted to be, which was a level 3 course". Notably, Abid and David share similar views of level 2 as a "stepping stone" to level 3. Comparatively, David positions level 2 qualifications within South College as serving a dual role for different types of learners.

David: I've seen it where you've actually ended up having two almost three streams of level 2s. Or you've had a group of students all of whom pretty much are intending to go into level 3 and the course is delivered in a slightly different way, you know almost as a precursor of that level 3. Then you've got another group who actually probably aren't gonna go into level 3 and want to go into employment, you're still doing the same qualification, but there's a twist given to it which allows them to progress into employment.

David's emphasis on level 2 as a "precursor" to level 3 contradicts Tyrone's experiences of repeating a level 2 qualification while supporting similar perceptions from Abid. David's positive framing of level 2 purpose and function contradicts broader academic and policy discussion which frames middle-track qualifications as reflective of a complicated and sometimes stratifying vocational framework.

What do learner narratives tell us about college-wide perceptions of media?

South's enrolment practices suggest that media studies were not valued within the college. Furthermore, the college's positioning of level 2 media as a progression catalyst for failed learners demonstrates a broader emphasis on the qualification rather than the subject. It can be argued that such attitudes reinforce assumptions of media studies as an "easy option" (Fraser and Wardle, 2013, p. 74). It is possible to conclude that South reflects the broader policy narrative in its marginalisation of media.

"I prefer it to school"

The learners shared similarly positive experiences of transitioning to FE. In Richard's case, this manifested in being treated like an adult. This was perhaps particularly important for Richard because of his negative school experiences, during which he felt as though he lacked voice and agency.

Richard: In college they talk to you as an adult like, you're on the same level as your peers and your teachers and it's a lot more friendly, like, um, you can, you can talk to teachers here about your problems and what's going on, you know.

Rachel measured her positive FE experiences with a positive learning environment. This seemed like an essential factor for Rachel, who had previously experienced negative relationships with schoolteachers.

Rachel: Doing the level 2 here rather than my GCSEs because I messed them up, made it happen for me. I was glad that I chose it, it was all full of genuinely nice people and all the teachers were nice. The way that it was taught and it is, the types of teachers here. Like I've never had a class that way in school. I do think that if I had maybe gone to a different college that the story might not have been the same.

Kate's transition into FE was less than seamless in comparison to her peers. Her absence from mainstream education for some years had compounded her lack of self-esteem.

Kate: It was weird because I hadn't been in school for like ages and it was weird to be back in an establishment or something. It sort of freaked out at but it was alright afterwards and then I liked how it was.

The decisive shift in Kate's transitional experiences implies a supportive FE environment, which enabled her to adjust to being back in education slowly. Richard, Rachel, and Kate's positive learning experiences in FE were helping them rebuild their self-esteem.

"It's different to GCSEs"

Kate, Rachel, and Tyrone emphasised the differences between FE and school learning. For Kate, this was reflected in attentive FE teachers and an individualised and interactive learning environment.

Kate: I liked how it was like very interactive instead of like sitting down and just reading a book and stuff like that. That's what I found so interesting about college because like with lectures here engage [and] want know who you are, instead of just "here's a book, why don't you just read for a bit". That's what I liked about it. I got to learn like everything including animation, which was cool because I've never done it before.

While Kate welcomed the change in learning, she presented broader retention issues within her cohort that reflect level 2 teaching reflections from Michael.

Kate: Well a lot of people dropped out [laughs] that's the first thing I noticed. But I liked it because you get to do like everything in the first year and I met a lot of interesting people ... but as I said there was only like three people left afterwards.

Level 2 media was providing a welcome change to a "pressurised" GCSE dynamic for Rachel, who disliked the GCSE exam culture. However, in contrast to the rest of the learners, Kate found similarities between her school and FE learning.

Kate: I think it's similar, some points of it except you don't have exams and stuff like that. But it's similar in some points because obviously you have like check-ups of what you've done which is sort of like exams and you do checks-ups of what you've done, evaluations. But like, not completely the same.

Comparatively, in making a distinction between GCSEs and the First Diploma, Rachel makes a difference between vocational and academic and demonstrates pride in the professional identity of the level 2 courses.

Rachel: I don't think it [level 2] is an alternative to GCSE because it's vocational, it has helped the way it's been taught here, I suppose I haven't had the experience anywhere else so [laughs] … but it's just the way it's been taught that is so different to GCSE. GCSE is so pressurised whereas with level 2 you get that support. I felt at ease, like looked after in a way.

Furthermore, in highlighting a lack in equivalency between level 2 and GCSEs, Rachel challenges qualification equivalency between low-level vocational and general qualifications in some areas. Rachel's emphasis on support indicates that this is a crucial learning feature for her. Her focus on being "at ease" and "looked after" reflect a nurturing FE environment that contrasts sharply with her school experiences. Comparatively, Tyrone's prior experience of BTEC level 2 in his secondary school sixth form enabled him to compare his vocational training across both sites. As discussed, his school-based vocational learning had proven to be a bureaucratic burden for Tyrone. In contrast, South appeared to be offering him a "completely different" experience.

Tyrone: The First Diploma [has] actually helped me in terms of starting off with Final Cut Pro and stuff like that. So it was actually completely different except for the, like the typing up and stuff, which here was just a small part of it [BTEC First Media], but there [secondary school] it was just computers through and through. So it isn't too bad.

Tyrone's experiences of vocational learning in school reinforce perspectives from South College principal David, who challenges the value, quality, and currency of professional training in secondary schools, and strongly position FE as the more experienced provider. Kate, Rachel, and Tyrone draw attention to the practical elements of the level 2 media. While Rachel emphasises a vocational identity for the course, Kate refers to the course's "interactivity", and Tyrone identifies opportunities for his digital skills enhancement. Unlike the other learners, Tyrone was also able to strike a comparison between his media learning at school and in college.

Tyrone: Okay, in media there [secondary school] like I would've learnt about stuff like form, audience, institution, presentation, ideology, which I did in Year 11 and the AS. But here it's more in terms of you just analyse stuff but not using those terms. So at that level it was more in terms of like learning every single part of media. So we learnt in detail, so I would say in school, even with English, it was more in detail cos I did GCSE English and it was a lot more different at the school level than here.

Tyrone's comparisons in his school and FE media learning suggest that his school was theory orientated. Tyrone also draws comparisons between FE and school pedagogy.

Tyrone: At the school level it was more like you learnt everything, then you still had to keep it in your head, go to the next level and you have to know it, then do it from there. Here [South College] it's more just like take it, do it yourself, so you have to be independent, you know. So there it was more like, although you were independent, you were given the fundamentals with media.

Tyrone references a more "detailed" delivery style that taught students the "fundamentals" in comparison to a less involved FE teaching style, which he describes as an independent form of learning. This implies that he had stronger teaching and learning experiences at school.

Tyrone: I would say well that's how you learn. You have to know something, then take it to the next level, then that's where you do it yourself. You don't really kind of expect everyone to be pushing you all the time.

Tyrone was able to rationalise both learning experiences and appears to have accessed something positive from both styles of learning. As his earlier reflections indicate, his exposure to new technologies at South provided him with skills he found valuable. Learners' experiences of level 2 learning as an alternative to GCSE represents FE as a second-chance provider.

Progression, aspirations, transitions, and destinations

For some learners, such as Abid, Kate, and Tyrone, the level 2 media held the promise of a second chance. For others, such as Rachel, Dominic, and Richard, their level 2 journey represented further failure.

"Doing and not doing" level 2

Richard de-enrolled shortly after securing a place on the course because of financial reasons. This would end up being his first out of two overall attempts at the level 2 media course.

Richard: I don't know, it just kind of went a bit fucked up really. Getting here is a problem, the college has no kind of funding for those people, I'm 19 and I live on my own and I get income support … at the moment I'm getting £27 a week and it cost me 20 quid on the train to get here. And there's no extra funding you can get to get here. So, it's either that or walk, ridiculous fucking walk there is.

Richard's situation is reflective of deeper underlying issues relating to social class and educational opportunity discussed in broader literature. Framing Richard's story within the 14–19 reformative frameworks, some critical issues begin to emerge. For Richard the college's policy enactment was resonating with his previous marginalisation within the school system, as, post-school expulsion, his entry into South College had been framed as a new beginning and a second chance at education. In retrospect, this was far removed from the realities of his life course at South, which was proving problematic to his long-term academic and professional development.

In parallel to Richard's narrative, Rachel and Dominic had undertaken and failed the level 2 media. Rachel attributed their failure to South College's disciplinary action, which at stage 3 for non-attendance and assessment submission had expelled her from the course.

Rachel: I got ill towards the end of the year so I weren't actually allowed to come to college. So I didn't actually finish it.

Rachel's initial experiences of level 2 can be dated back to a pre-merger South College. The strong disciplinary action that she experienced at South represents a different departmental culture to the one that Michael shares some years later. The contrast in Rachel's earlier experiences and Michael's later accounts of "special measures" and a relaxed disciplinary system is indicative of a decline in departmental structures and processes. Dominic rationalised his level 2 failures in the context of his GCSE outcomes and as a representation of his lack of work ethic and positioned the experience as useful for later life.

Dominic: I imagine if I had got the grades I'd wanted it would have meant that as a person I would have been a lot more hardworking. I probably would have ended up finishing the course and then going on to doing level 3 here. I think realistically I would have had a completely different lifestyle, but it wouldn't have necessarily been what I wanted to the level 2 course here I wouldn't have been able to have done it, so I think really it prepared me sort of mentally and being aware of how much work needs to be done and how to sort of organise myself and time management.

Dominic's emphasis on a lack of interest in media suggests that his motivations for the study were centred on subject satisfaction rather than progression through the levels. As he suggests in his earlier accounts, his assumptions of what media would entail differed from the realities. Dominic's linkage between his failure at level 2 and GCSE suggests that his academic self-conceptualisation still linked strongly to his school experiences.

In contrast to the rest of the learners, Dominic did not continue his study at South College post level 2. He experienced a three-year period of unemployment and was classified as NEET. Dominic's post level 2 narratives ran parallel to Rachel's, who was also identified as NEET.

The absence of industry links within vocational media training limits learners' professional opportunities within the media industry. Richard problematises this lack of media industry exposure within vocational qualifications.

Richard: They, they can start off by actually showing what it's like, we have trips out but we've never actually had trips out to go and see what it's like, you know, go and see what an actual set is like and what the working conditions are. That could help, you know.

To summarise, these were learners that had failed their GCSEs, were creatively inclined, presented SpLDs or behavioural issues, or were classified as of low academic ability based on their educational outcomes at school. In comparison to the other learners, Kate and Abid experienced a comparatively seamless transition from level 2 to 3 media, while Tyrone made sustained attempts at being moved up a level.

Tyrone: When we first got here in September, one of my other classmates in my class, she had the same problem. So we both went to our tutor. I did bring it up that I'd actually applied in time and went in for the interview in time too. My tutor said that it was because the National Diploma course was already filled up. But at that time they didn't actually tell me that the National Diploma course was filled up, they told me that I didn't have enough qualifications. I thought he could've did more, like trying to solve it more. I didn't chase it up after that.

Tyrone's experiences represent many issues within the media department at the time. The lack of tutor support in resolving his issues contradicts David's vision of pastorally supportive level 2 frameworks at South College.

David: Level 2 students are often more needy in terms of support needs. Not necessarily in terms of learning support, but you know have sort of typical teenage issues or problems at home. So, a good tutor that understands level 2s and understands their needs is crucial.

It is possible to conclude that Tyrone's situation was a result of the pressures that the department was under. The media department's high staff turnover, restructures, staff redundancies, and a lack of middle and curriculum management were crucial issues affecting the area at the time. Drawing on South College's eco narrative, it is possible to identify a causal relationship between the department's instability and Tyrone's experiences. Furthermore, the college's emphasis on targets and funding suggests that the student recruitment practices at South were centred on filling courses. As Tyrone asserts, his place on the level 3 was linked to places on the course rather than entry criterion. Taking these contexts into consideration, it is possible to infer that Tyrone's steer onto the level 2 was motivated by the funding he would bring into the college rather than his long-term welfare and progression. Richard and Rachel re-joined the level 2 media three years apart, aged 19. Rachel returned to the department as it experienced its most turbulent times, post-merger. She noted the differences in her level 2 learning and struck comparisons.

Rachel: Comparing the two courses, the two, because they are very different [to] what I did before and now. I suppose in a way this course, this one was better but in other ways it wasn't. I suppose this year has been in certain ways I have felt supported, like certain teachers have helped me and shown me how to do things, they have actually spent time to do it. Whereas in other elements I feel like not just me but the whole class been completely just been left and feel lost.

Rachel's experiences of the First Diploma in 2006 and 2009 offer a stark contrast of changes within the department. Her comparison between the two courses represents a decline in the quality of learning and teaching on level 2. The department's instability as cited by Michael is reflected in Rachel's experiences of a lack of overall support on the course. By separating her experience across teachers, Rachel captures the divisions within the department that Michael references, reflecting a less standardised and holistic learning experience in comparison to her experiences in 2006.

Rachel: So …I know other groups have had worse but we have been messed around in certain things. Like before I had set teachers, they were with us for a whole year whereas like this [year] I felt a little bit lost in certain subjects. Like media theory, I still don't know what is going on and what I need to actually do. I suppose media theory in general [laughs], it's just too confusing. I know it's not about your classmates, but the class hasn't been as great as it has been previously [laughs].

Rachel's experience suggests that the course in 2009 was fragmented concerning style and content in its delivery. Moreover, her reference to feeling supported in some areas while not in others suggests a variation in pedagogy and support across the course. The departmental narrative of the time suggests that Rachel's experiences were linked to management restructure, a high volume of new hourly paid staff teaching on courses, and the launch of the new BTEC First Diploma media specification.

Richard was also retaking the level 2 media at the same time but in a different cohort to Rachel. Like Rachel, he also noted a decline in the quality of the provision.

Richard: When I came here to begin with, it seems to me that it was lot better here then what it is now. They seem to be a lot more helpful. It seems to just be going

> downhill if you know what I mean? I don't really
> know like what the difference is you lot have made
> to making me [feel] like that but it just seems to me
> that it's that way – but when I first came here it was
> lot more helpful.

Richard's observations of a decline within the department and a lack of support resonate with Rachel's experiences at the same time. However, it is possible to argue that Richard's experiences were perhaps more severe in respect to the quality of his learning experiences.

Richard: For a start the teachers this year some moved but, I mean, we've still got a couple of good teachers, like Connor who was a brilliant teacher but he is a bit long sometimes but he knows what he's going on about. We had six changeovers in teachers which is ridiculous and not good enough … like every time a teacher changed all the work that we done with the previous teacher, we were just told "that's rubbish, what they told you was wrong and throw it in the bin", so we've had to do the year's-worth of work like six times. So I don't understand how they expect us to do that, it's like not possible. The deadline for the entire course is today and people have still only done a quarter of their work. So it's a bit out of order really.

Richard's experiences reflect negative impacts of staff turnover on his learning. His emphasis on Connor as a "brilliant" teacher suggests that more experienced lecturers within the department were able to provide a productive learning experience for learners. It is possible to argue that Richard's experiences perhaps become more prevalent in the context of his early history with South College. As a former 14-plus learner, Richard had a long history with South. The support that he had received at South had been one of the strengths of his experience. The decline he notes echoes his previous negative school experiences. His reference to not knowing why his quality of learning had declined at South suggests that, although learners were able to identify the quality of their learning experience, they held limited knowledge of institutional and departmental systems.

In striking comparison between Richard and Rachel's former and "present" (during the research timeframe) experiences of South, it is possible to conclude that college ecologies are complex and can vary based on the circumstances and the individuals involved. Their exposures defined these learners' former experiences to media during their earlier time at South. Their "current" experiences reflect a shift in South's ecology to a less stable learning environment than they had previously experienced. Contrary to a notable decline in his overall learning experience, Richard noted that his quality of learning support was excellent. However, he emphasised its lack of standardisation across the college and questioned its need in his level 2 classes.

Richard: Personally I think I get help [from] teachers and stuff like that come in and, you know, help like. They generally help the class, they're not specifically for me, but I reckon there's a lot of places round the college that need it a lot more than like my class, do you know what I mean like? Like catering doesn't get it but there are like quite a few like dyslexic children

> in catering. I do get help but I don't think I need it as much as some people do.

Except for Dominic, the learners completed the level 2 and progressed onto the National Diploma (level 3) media course at South College. In this respect, FE had awarded these learners their second chance by enabling educational transitions post GCSE failure. It can be argued that South College continued to perform its second-chance FE function despite challenging policy-levered change. Furthermore, learners' successful transition into level 3 suggest that South's policy ecology, though unstable, was still maintaining positive learning cultures that were benefitting GCSE-failed learners aiming for educational progression. Richard's level 3 progression suggests continued serendipity in the South College student enrolment and recruitment process.

Richard: I don't know what grade. I never got told what grade it was [for the level 2], but it must have been alright cos I got onto the National Diploma, media [at] South College.

However, Richard problematised his aspirations for level 3 progression, hence indicating an emerging disaffection that was similar to his school years.

Richard: As if I'm going to get anywhere else. South College is like the equivalent to those schools that everyone went to when you get expelled from your first school and nowhere else would take you, South College is the equivalent place for retards and fuck-ups. [I'm] more of a fuck-up than a retard ... I'd probably still come to South College because of the people at the time that came here because it's better than going to College A or College B. College A is just for wankers and everyone in College B [is] really posh, they're fucking hideous, hideous people, shouldn't exist.

Furthermore, his opinions on the South College ecology reflect his disillusionment with its second-chance function. Richard's aspirations at South College reflect an urgent will to progress underpinned by his feelings of academic "hopelessness" (Opsal, 2011, p. 159).

Richard: I have to finish this course. I haven't got a choice. Because I can't not finish it now that I've got on it and not only that, right, I want to go to uni next year.

Richard's positive appraisals of South College appear to have taken a downturn by the time he reaches the end of his level 2 qualifications some five years after he had initially joined the college as a 14-plus learner. His emphasis on not having a "choice" implicates a counterproductive progression system, in which his academic opportunities and access are limited.

Richard's post-college aspirations of progressing to university appear to have been his main drive for progressing onto the level 3. Richard's aspirations for progression onto a practical degree suggest that he was self-identifying as a vocational learner. He frames university as a similar alternative to FE, in performing a second-chance function.

Richard: It would have to be a practical degree. I'm not stupid, I don't think I'm going to get on a uni course and then immediately and be able to get a job with that cos it's based on who you know. But I actually want to learn more about the industry and if I go to uni I can do that. There must be someone who can teach me something new. To do that I have to get this course [level 3].

Richard's perceptions of what it takes to enter the media industry are linked to networking and contacts as opposed to academic progression. The value he places on a university course is pedagogic rather than as a catalyst for media employment.

While Richard positions levels 2 and 3 as progression catalysts to a university degree, Tyrone's post level 2 progression discussion is connected to remaining in the media discipline.

Tyrone: I'm most likely to stick with media since I've started media. Although I've heard a few other people say media is not good for the future for jobs and stuff, cos there's too many people getting into media, I still like media as a whole so I don't see myself getting out of it. Although like I said I do like business although it's hard, I still do like it. So if there is a course which includes the two together, I would like to do that.

Tyrone's aspirations to "stick with media" appear to be somewhat hindered by concerns for future industry employment. Tyrone's rationale for not taking business implies that he finds media to be a more comfortable option. Except for Dominic, the learners expressed an aim to progress onto level 3, suggesting aspirations of progressing through the levels. This was also evident in learners' final South College interviews as they approached the end of their studies. Dominic, who had spent four years as NEET, transitioned into a hairdressing apprenticeship.

Dominic: I went back and forth and then I have sort of got back into education. I am doing NVQ in hairdressing with **** [leading high street hairdressing chain], an actual salon. It was a choice that I'd made just cos I wanted to sort of do a bit of travelling and there's a lot of places that are prepared to give visas to people who do hairdressing.

Dominic's motivation for undertaking the apprenticeship reflects limited long-term career planning. Dominic's post GCSE failure pathway represents the messy trajectory that Wolf (2011) and Atkins (2013) caution against. In this theme, Dominic's transition into apprenticeship was brief as he transitioned again into low-level vocational training.

Dominic: I was there for less than six months and they turned around and said, you're too old now, we don't want you anymore. I was, possibly 20.

After some uncertainty, Dominic appears to have found a discipline that he felt passionate about, in animal husbandry. His training in this area manifested through a successful volunteering experience at a wildlife sanctuary and subsequent vocational training at a different FE college (anonymised as College A in Richard's earlier discussion).

Dominic: I was working for wildlife here for quite a bit and I was promoted to supervisor. I was the youngest person they'd ever had as a supervisor. Obviously it was still a charity so I wasn't getting paid. So I [thought] well this is obviously something that I should probably try and push.

Voluntary work with a wildlife charity had enabled him to discover an interest and motivate further study. It could be argued that work experience opportunities can play a decisive role in enabling learner career choice. For Dominic, aimlessness was perhaps a necessary period to find the direction, and his persistence potentially created opportunities for him to find a vocational direction. In parallel to the media learners, Dominic transitioned onto a BTEC Level 3 Animal Management Extended Diploma in 2012. The youngest from within the sample, Dominic's journey to level 3 had taken the longest. It can be argued that Dominic's second chance was still fulfilled by FE.

"I'm on the National Diploma"

Learner experiences of level 3 were varied. Abid, Richard, and Rachel joined the course as the department was collapsing its specialist National Diploma strands and adopting a generic specification approach. The decision was motivated by the lecturer make-up of the department and individuals' personal teaching preferences for specific units. Information regarding the collapse did not reach applicants till registration week. Learners Rachel, Richard, and Abid expressed a mixture of views on the collapse of the National Diploma specialist pathways.

Abid: I applied for the journalism one initially … which I'm kind of glad got changed because it's not really something I want to be going into, you know.

Rachel: One thing I didn't like is that this college used to do specialisms so used to have a television and film course, and now you don't have that and I feel that the publishing and journalism has been sort of left behind.

Richard: I don't think that's right that they can change it after you've applied for it. I applied cos they were three separate courses. They combined them without informing us until the first day of term. So I think that's a little bit unfair as well.

The lack of departmental consultation with applicants before making the change demonstrates marginalisation of learners' voices.

Dominic's transition to level 3 seemed comparatively seamless. Dominic emphasised the challenging, high-quality learning he was receiving at College "A".

Dominic: The assignments are laid out to reach pass, merit or distinction targets and you have criterias that gets harder and harder. If you're going for the distinction levels you have to do everything off your own back essentially. You're not allowed to have any help from tutors – in the past two years I've done 70 assignments and I've got two folders of my work that are just like that thick. Looking at them now I'm like, oh my God how did I do that much, but yeah I think if I tried to do this course back when I did this level 2 course here, I wouldn't have been able to have done it. I think for me it was definitely better going to somewhere more structured.

Dominic's experiences reflect a significant shift in his attitudes to learning. This can in part be linked to the pressures of age and increasingly limited opportunity and, in part, to his interest in the subject that he moves onto. His focus on "structure" suggests his need for clear frameworks and guidance. His experience suggests that "structure" was lacking in his past learning. This shift in Dominic's narrative suggests a positive shift in his academic self-concept over time. Comparatively, the media sample also expressed an assignment-heavy level 3 learning experience. In contrast to Dominic, some learners criticised the course structure delivery as unsupportive and overly dependent on learners' independent learning and essay-writing skills.

Dominic: The course learning, from what I can tell it's just what you know already. You don't get taught anything. It's just you're expected to like know already. It's not challenging. There's no need for all the writing. If they want me to make something why do I need this huge fucking paper trail to go with it? There's a huge like checklist that I was like oh, Jesus Christ. Essay on this, essay on that. Three thousand words on describing advertisements? – fuck off! I don't care! I'd like to learn something new now and again cos that's the whole point isn't it really?

Rachel: It was quite a gap. The main difference I found is that you've got to have all this paperwork and I didn't like the fact that in the first year it was like, oh there's not that much work, then in second year it was like essay, essay, essay [laughs].

Abid: I think that's the problem with it, at the end of the day it's a bit too independent and you tend to become a bit more lazy. Like there were some issues with attendance and working, but that's purely because of the fact that I wasn't motivated.

Richard and Abid's learning experiences echo Tyrone's earlier emphasis on the "independent learning" vocational pedagogy within the department. For these learners, this style of learning was non-conducive to their educational enhancement.

Richard: Our teacher for video came in and [said] there you are, have a play about with the software and everyone was like, what the fuck is this? – And he was like "shit, I have to teach them how to use this and there's like 25 of them and there are like so many days to teach them". So he asked me to give him a hand during class, and so I taught like half the class how to use the software, doing him a favour. I think the only reason he chose me is cos to be fair I'm quite handy on it. There's no support, there's no interaction at all.

For Richard, independent learning evolved into peer teaching. The emphasis on essay writing indicates an A Level style coursework model, which counteracts vocational approaches. His experiences support criticisms from Buckingham (2017) of an academicised vocational media system. Linking his experiences to earlier references to wanting to learn "something new", it is possible to conclude that Richard's video class dynamic was counterproductive to his learning. In assisting his teacher as a "favour", Richard was being deprived of opportunities for learning development. However, another strand to this discourse emerges when framed in the policy enactment of South's media department. It can be argued that the instability and staff turnover was affecting the quality of learning experiences for media learners at the time. In these circumstances, teachers may tend to theorise the subject and restrict learners' opportunities to engage in practical work. Linking this point to Richard's experiences, it can be argued that both the quality and currency of vocational media education is inconsistent and thus problematic in the context of skills and chances policy rhetoric.

For instance, Connor appears to be in favour of academic approaches to teaching vocational media, while Michael's teaching appears to be more technically and creatively focused. In contrast to Richard and Abid, some learners like Kate shared an emerging interest in theoretical work and a preference for writing over practical.

Kate: I think I am better at theory because I like exploring stuff and like researching about it, but practical is always fun but I like knowing more about the subject than just like continually filming.

Richard's position on the level 3 came under threat as he continued to experience financial difficulties. He talked a lot about his negative experiences of poor tutoring, teaching, and peer dynamics. His experiences demonstrate that these issues were impacting on his learning access and development.

Richard: I went to go and see my tutor because it's gone past the end of the year. [In] my last disciplinary they said that I could come in whenever I can because of money troubles. They said don't worry about the other stuff for the minute, just worry about getting the final major project done and then once that's done then you can worry about the rest of the stuff afterwards during the summer holidays. I just went to ask her [for the] certain date and she was like, "you get an extra week". It's ridiculous, she's given it to everyone. She's like, "you have to get it done by this date otherwise we haven't got enough time to mark it".

The tutor can be seen to represent the power that individuals hold in FE to shape the experiences of young people. Richard perceived her interactions as unsupportive and in conflict with the pastoral role that she was serving as his tutor. In this sense, Richard's experiences of a lack of support can be linked directly to a pedagogue's self-positioning in the learning environment as opposed to broader factors. Richard was beginning to demonstrate a growing awareness of class divisions within his class, which represented elements of the broader social issues that were affecting him.

Richard: College is shit. It's full of middle-class wankers who have no fucking idea what they're going on about any of the time. They're happy enough to sit there and run their mouths all fucking day about this and that and their daddy's Jaguar and their new riding ponies. It's shut the fuck up. I don't need to hear it. You just come in and you're starving … I had no fucking breakfast. Some cunt's sat there going, oh, I've got a new pony this morning. Good for you, dick head!

Richard felt that social class divisions among his peers were a reproduction of their school social groups. Richard paints a picture in which age and course levels at college had not prevented young people reconnecting with their former school peers to replicate their silos or social class framings as he had experienced in school. It is possible to conclude that this dynamic may have emerged as a result of an uncertain departmental landscape, which was motivating media learners to re-form familiar alliances and groups. It can also be argued that Richard's experiences were representing a conflict between the interconnectedness of a cohort and his social self. As his responses indicate, he was negotiating social class with previously adverse school exposures to peer groups, while studying at South.

Richard: The trouble is, though, all the new people that came from school came from these people's schools. So they went oh, bloody, you're kind, you're only a couple of years above me. And you know falling into the same group of fucking retards.

If this was the case, from Richard's perspective, the media department was becoming increasingly school-like. After nearly seven years at the college, Richard was unable to complete the National Diploma. Richard's South College outcome can in part be mapped to his financial issues and, in part, to South's turbulent narrative and 14–16 policy creative arts qualifications. The earlier policy had positioned him into a framework of the pre-entry low-level vocational provision that functioned as a barrier to his academic progression and compounded the issues arising from his lower socio-economic status. It can be argued that the lack of communications between faculty subdivisions and a fragmented media teaching team was impacting directly on the quality of Richard's learning and his accessibility to opportunity. The media department's turbulent dynamic appears to have compounded Richard's frustrations, and he demonstrates increasing disaffection.

Richard: I have called pretty much every teacher in this college a cunt at least once – they're all cunts. My stupid class, they're all wankers. Who then take the piss out of the way I speak and make like Facebook groups about it. The entire class made a Facebook group about me with really badly Photoshopped pictures of me to look like Marilyn Monroe and stuff.

Richard's increasing disaffectedness begins to represent his negative school personas. Was this perhaps because the issues he raises about his school learning were being echoed in his later South College experience? If so, what factors could this be attributed to?

Richard: I don't have any personal anguish, just a class barrier. Well they were just trying to stick me really ain't they? To be fair. Because I'm not well liked by these particular teachers.

Richard's experiences implicate feelings of exclusion, bullying, and a lack of agency. It can be argued that these dynamics were triggering earlier negative behaviours from his school years. In contrast to these learners, Rachel and Kate's experiences of the level 3 were favourable, as both learners prepared for progression to university.

Rachel: I am glad I did this course anyway because I wouldn't know what to go onto next. I've got 19 distinctions so I've got the highest that they've had here. In September I applied for a few uni courses but I got onto the one I wanted, which is good. I'm going to UCA in Farnham and doing a Bachelors [in] Advertising and Brand Communication, because I think it hones in my skills of media.

Kate: [I progressed onto the] National Diploma, which is like two years is in movie image. And in September I'm starting erm university … [doing a] three-year [BA] course in media and communications.

These learners shared similar outcomes to Tyrone, who had also made a successful progression into higher education. It is possible to assert that these learners had realised their second chance in FE and that South College has restored them from GCSE failed learners with negative school experiences. In comparison, Abid also realised his second chance in successfully attaining his level 3 qualification. Although he had shared aspirations for progression to university, he did not apply via the UCAS process.

"After college I want to …"

Framing some learners' level 3 media engagement with their long-term career aspirations, it is possible to identify a continued interest in media.

Tyrone: I like to aim high but I don't wanna make it too high cos I've started telling myself nah, that's really hard to get that, but um, I'd love to get something along the role of directing, editing, along those things.

Rachel: I've [thought about] going into accounting. So

advertising would incorporate all the skills that I've learnt here and that I already possess.

Richard: I really want to [film] direct. I know that I couldn't actually be a director, I couldn't just go and be like I've got all these degrees, can I have a job please, cos it doesn't work that way to be honest. I just … I'm going to be using this as a way of knowing more about the industry so when I get into it I actually know what I'm doing.

In contrast to these learners, Rachel connected her media aspirations to her interests in accountancy. Richard and Tyrone shared cautious aspirations of careers in the media industry. The caution represented by both learners suggests an awareness of a competitive media industry. Kate's responses were comparatively ambiguous, as she disclosed a lack of certainty for the future. Her position on an academic media degree represented a lack of interest in pursuing a media trade, though she did express an interest in producing.

Kate: I have no idea. I hope I am going to figure it out in the first year. [I would like to be a] producer as I know how to like bring it altogether.

Learner generalised responses demonstrated a lack of career direction, as their chosen South College paths had not trained them for a specific role in the industry (Buckingham, 2017). In contrast to the rest of the learners, Abid connected his initial aspirations for academic progression to social and familial pressures, suggesting a broader ecology at play that was beyond the scope of South.

Abid: My parents are from Bangladesh and they come here and they believe that education is key and vital in progression of life. In a way I also see that, I never used to see that, but now I understand that. I didn't really want to go [to university] myself. I would say [it was because of] social pressures as in my parents wanting me to go to university.

Not continuing in his education represents Abid overcoming his pressures and moving towards making his own choices. However, South College did provide him with the tools that he needed to make the progression into higher education should he have decided to. In this context, South College had fulfilled its role for Abid.

"What happened to me after South College"

When asked to reflect on the possible impacts that policymakers may have had on his life, like Connor, Richard did not differentiate between political parties or broader and more localised contexts.

Richard: I'm kind of glad New Labour's out. I know this, the majority of my life I was getting stuck by those. It doesn't matter whose, which puppet. You're still getting fucked over no matter what they're calling themselves.

Richard's financial situation worsened, and he has continued to shift between long periods of unemployment and homelessness.

Richard: I'm still skint [laughs]. Well they'll cut my benefits by

the end of the year easily and it will just get worse.
Like today for instance there's no leccy [electricity] at
my house. Get out the door, have you got any money?
No. Have you got any money? But life goes on. It's all
bollocks really, isn't it? Life in general. Life's bollocks. I
fear for the future.

Richard's feeling of early disaffection and hopelessness appear
to have continued into adulthood. His financial situation appears
to have worsened as he became increasingly reliant on the
state. It can be argued that, although South had performed an
intermediary second-chance function for Richard after school,
the qualifications he had attained at South were bringing him
little long-term value. While his situation can be attributed to a
range of factors beyond South's policy enactment of the 14–19
frameworks, it is possible to conclude that policy levers such
as changes to FE funding (for Richard this manifested in the
withdrawal of the education maintenance allowance (EMA)
and his lack of access to free further education post 19) and an
unstable department did act as barriers to his ability to sustain
a place at South. However, there is no evidence to suggest that,
had Richard remained at South, he would have transitioned
into further education or employment. In some respects, his
own attitudes of disaffection can be argued as having acted as
bigger barriers to him. Although he was experiencing a range
of pressures, which he attributed to his socio-economic status,
Richard demonstrated a lesser motivation to succeed in his
studies by the time he had reached level 3. His motivation to
learn differed significantly from many of the other learners in this
sense, such as Rachel and Dominic, who had both re-engaged

with their education after a period of disruption. Another angle to this discussion suggests that Richard's academic self-concept had not evolved or developed since his initial failure at school. This may explain his continued references to these experiences and the parallels that he draws between South College and his former school.

After South, Abid spent some time out of employment and training and settled working in the family restaurant business. Abid's narrative provides insights into the interconnectedness of an individual's ecology, and while educational experiences do assist in shaping a person's development, these form one of many elements within a broader social ecosystem. The interconnectedness of exposure, experience, and networks can all have a lasting effect on shaping an individual's life and experiences. Kate, who had represented the most robust progression potential at the beginning of the study, did not continue in her university education after falling pregnant. Instead, she has since been focusing on raising her son and, during the last check-in, identified as a single mum.

In academic and progression terms, Tyrone, Dominic, and Rachel were the most successful learners among the young people in this study. Post South, Tyrone progressed onto a foundation degree programme at a different institution and followed an engineering and, later, information systems path at university. Tyrone reflects positively on his South experiences and frames his college learning as an integral driver in assisting his transition to university.

Tyrone: My university experience was a complete new world of experiences, majorly from an educational perspective and furthermore in shaping me for the real world. My educational experience at university was a steep learning curve cause of the complete change of curriculum from media/design to engineering, which made the first year just as challenging as the final year. In all of this because of the vast exposure to learning strategies and levels I had at South College, not to mention the help I received from tutors, I was able to adjust accordingly to the major change of curriculums.

He is currently employed within an IT company and had this to say about his experiences at South and their impact on his current life:

Tyrone: During my time at college I was a design subject. The tutoring I received during the course of the time at South, I developed not only knowledge at different levels that I still use till this very day, but also skills of adaptation because of the learning regimes, which were a big step ahead of my previous experience in sixth form and were the perfect preparation for university. Needless to say again, my overall experience at South played a vital part in taking me to the next step, leading me to where I am now and it's mostly all thanks to the support I received from tutors. which pushed me out of my comfort zone to chase something that didn't then seem a reality.

Tyrone's experiences at South appear to have been productive in the long term. In his retrospective reflections, he can identify the value of the learning he received at South in enabling him to transition to university. Like Tyrone, Rachel also changed academic direction, initially enrolling on to an advertising degree and then changing to architecture. Rachel graduated in 2017 and, like Abid, currently works for the family decorating business. Unlike Tyrone, Rachel's experiences at South did not adequately equip her for university study.

Rachel: BTEC definitely prepared me for a practical course, it did somewhat prepare me for the style of working, as I was on a Bachelor of Arts which is a vocational course as well – but I did feel I was not properly assisted in understanding what course would suit my skills. I chose BA advertising that I really didn't like, as I misunderstood what it was as such due to our course teaching it differently. It was completely different to how we were taught at South and so that did make me struggle and I ended up changing my course after the first year. I went on to do BA in interior architecture and design. Which strangely enough had more transferable skills than the advertising.

Dominic graduated with a degree in animal behaviour and welfare in 2016 from college A. He currently works as a dog carer and driving assistant at a dog adventure company. In these three instances, these young people can be identified as educationally successful. However, their post South trajectory represents a similar messiness to their post-school transitions. Framing this in the context of their media education, it can be argued that, while the level 2 media course enabled educational progression for these learners, it did not serve a bigger vocational purpose in line with policy rhetoric. As Rachel reflects, her first degree in a similar discipline did not complement her media learning at South. This raises concerns about the role of vocational media learning.

Did South College give me a second chance?

Richard, Rachel, and Dominic all experienced a sustained period of unemployment after leaving South College. This point is particularly prevalent in Rachel and Richard's case, as these students had been participating in a range of pre-vocational programmes at the college, which had arguably brought them little market value. However, once these learners had framed vocational level 2 as a progression route onto the level 3, they were able to make successful transitions into further education. It is, therefore, possible to argue that the function of level 2 and subsequently low-level vocational courses are not clear-cut and are dependent on a range of factors such as the individual, college ecology, and policy narrative. For instance, in Dominic's case, he was able to use the level 2 successfully to his advantage at other institutions to educationally progress. As he confirmed, it was level 2 media and, subsequently, South College that wasn't right for him. Similarly, Rachel also engaged with a range of routes before opting to retake the level 2 as a means of progression onto higher qualifications. This worked well for her, as she was able to progress through the levels successfully. These narratives represent the power that an individual can hold.

South College's role as a second-chance provider was varied for these learners. While for some, such as Tyrone, Rachel, Abid, and Kate, South enabled access to opportunities and progression, in Richard's case South's second-chance function is more complex. While he was given a series of opportunities to access learning over a sustained period, his disciplinary-levered level 3 outcome so close to the end of his two-year studies counteracted some of the excellent work that South had done.

In conclusion, it is possible to identify commonalities within the personal narratives of South College staff and learners.

The nuanced academic narratives presented by these young people represent the systemic marginalisation of learners identified as non-academic, low ability, or with learning disabilities. Learners' damaging stories of marginalisation echoed Michael's experiences of being a "slow" dyslexic learner. David supports the view of FE as a positive shift for failed learners wishing to pursue academic study.

Learners' experiences of vocational study at school were mostly negative. Their stories present schools as unequipped to provide good-quality vocational training. David endorsed this view in his emphasis on the vocational strengths of FE and questioned the credentials of schoolteachers in teaching vocational qualifications because of their perceived lack of industry experience.

The vocational and academic divide was prevalent in the participants' stories and, like Michael, all learners self-classified as practical, as opposed to academic.

Like the learners, Michael also shared experiences of GCSE failure and negative school experiences and linked his earlier feelings of failure to his early feelings of low self-esteem. Michael's academic narrative represents a process of negotiation similar to the learners. Over time, Michael was able to rebuild his self-esteem and overcome some of the damaging learning experiences he had experienced in school; however, it is uncertain whether he was able to offer meaningful or ethical teaching and learning experiences to any of his learners, given the young people's accounts.

Older learners such as Richard, Rachel, and Kate can also take inspiration from Connor's and David's narratives of returning to study and changing careers later in life. Contrary to the dynamic presented by their schools of failure and success, David and Connor were not defined by their messy journeys and were able to successfully navigate their education as mature students and demonstrate a positive example of lifelong learning.

4
What can we learn?

I embarked on this project with several areas of focus and some questions. I was mostly interested in learning more about the experiences of negatively classified learners directly from them, and to understand the impact classifying had on learners. Over the course of my study, I was able to see the long-lasting damage that negative classifications can have and how this can impact on learners. This provided a backdrop to two key questions:

- Were educators and institutional management sharing the same vision of the learning, teaching, and support they were providing young people?
- Were teaching staff equipped and adequately supported to deliver specialist courses such as media studies?

The answer to both questions was a "no". Staff accounts reflected a lack of synchronicity in their visions of teaching, learning, and support. Teaching staff saw themselves as separate from management while managers saw themselves as leading the institution with a shared vision that all staff were invested in. Furthermore, beginning teachers were underequipped and unprepared, and established lecturers felt underdeveloped and held back from career progression. Teacher training systems and structures also seemed to work in a deficit, whereby staff like

Michael, who had no prior teaching experience, were able to secure a space on a training programme for experienced staff.

Learning objective: What can we learn?

- To encourage schools, colleges, and pupil referral students to centralise learner voice and use this to inform practices on an ongoing basis.

As this research shows, a range of external factors influenced South College, its staff, and, subsequently, its students. The findings suggest that policy churn and financial instability were important themes to emerge from South's policy enactment which subsequently affected learners directly and indirectly. This can be understood through the lens of qualification reform and departmental restructuring and the impact of this on learners' college experiences. The study indicates that individuals were often caught in a reactionary dynamic in the absence of advanced information, strategies, or due warning before change. This can be seen in Tyrone's recruitment narrative and Richard's disciplinary action(s). Significantly, connections between broader institutional narratives and teacher and learners could be identified in their classroom exchanges. This was mainly the case where the learners were performing a reciprocal role in the mediation process within the teaching and learning exchange. For instance, Richard's subtle interaction was captured in assisting his lecturer through peer teaching technical media, in response to a shortage of teaching staff and large class sizes, suggesting that Richard was experiencing the indirect impacts of an overwhelmed department. Some learners, such as Richard and Rachel, could identify changes within South's ecology based on their prior exposures; however, there was little evidence that learners had an overall awareness of South's narratives.

The media learning experiences of the young people in this case presented as mixed. In many cases, such as for Richard, Abid, Rachel, and Tyrone, this could be linked to South's inconsistent teaching and learning.

This is most visible in the differences of perception between staff; for example, there was little evidence from the lecturers' accounts that David was aware of feelings on the ground among staff. Although David attempted to connect the different strands of enactment in his discussion of national policy mediation, remaining staff and young people discussed a self-orientated view of enactment and did not join up the different strands of activity in the college to form a broader sense of the institution. Lecturer and learner accounts appeared critical of some of South's practices and disassociated themselves from perceived bad practice. An example of this can be seen in the difference between David and teaching staff's perceptions of what was happening "on the ground". David asserted a positive shift in South's culture, while Connor and Michael shared less-than-positive views on departmental cultures and practices. Connor's references to a positive past institutional culture also contradicted David's framing of South's past practices. In the learners' case, this manifested in some learners, such as Abid and Kate, critiquing the quality of teaching and learning on the level 3.

South was lacking a sense of community at the time of this research. David's numerous references to coming in temporarily to fix a problem with the college positioned him as an external representative and his status as an interim manager positioned him on the outside of the institution. Comparatively, the lecturers in this study positioned themselves as lacking in agency in the college enactment process. Learner narratives indicated that the lecturers were more active in the policy mediation process than they perceived because of their associations with a department that was experiencing change. Hence, they were often mediating change because of their position within the department. Significantly, lecturer accounts aligned closely together, as did learners with each other. This was indicative of unified experiences for different actor groups that had similar exposures or were performing similar enactment. In the following sections of this chapter, I will be discussing some of the key themes to have emerged from this study.

Long-term impacts of negative classifications on learners

There is currently limited research into the reasons why learners fail their GCSEs or disengage from their schooling before taking their examinations. In providing contexts to learners' failures in school, this research has elicited some commonalities of experience across the learners. These findings suggest that:

- Learners' schooling cultures strongly influenced their academic progress and attainment;
- Negative school cultures revealed hegemonic practices in

the classification and subsequent segregation of learners from the mainstream community of their school. This could be linked to learners' learning disabilities, behavioural issues, and perceived low academic ability;

- Learners felt a loss of their individuality within their schools. Some learners connected this to schooling approaches that were generic and standard driven; and

- Learners did not have adequate access to information and guidance relating to their academic choices and the effect that these would have on their long-term outcomes in school. Post-school, many learners engaged in a broadly unguided process of identifying and applying for courses.

Learner experiences suggest that "low ability" and "non-academic" classifications experienced in school followed young people for much of their educational lives. This was particularly prevalent in the cases of Dominic, Rachel, and Richard, whereby these learners navigated "messy trajectories" (Wolf, 2011, p. 39) amid a complicated vocational landscape and at points performed their classification roles (Buckingham, 2008). This is reflected at various points in all learner accounts as they self-identified as technically orientated and averse to "academic" courses. In Rachel's and Dominic's cases, this can be seen as manifesting in their failure at level 2 media and former disengagement with their FE studies, compounding their low-ability status, while in Richard's case his deteriorating experiences at South triggered a reenactment of his former school disaffection and associated behaviours. In these three instances, learners identified as NEET at various points, hence reinforcing the broader policy narrative for learners classified as low ability, learning disabled, or disaffected.

A critical issue to emerge from this study has been Tyrone's steering into middle-track media qualifications by the college recruitment team. On one level this steering reflected broader dynamics at the college, while, on another level, a broader policy-driven narrative of marginalisation can be identified. Tyrone was subjected to unintended marginalisation to emerge out of potentially inefficient student recruitment and information systems; however, as the only Black young person in this study with the highest attainment at the point of level 2, his steering at enrolment implies racist connotations.

The fragmented trajectories of learners in this study indicate a connection between GCSE failure and a lack of social mobility. Considering this, questions arise concerning the connections between middle-track qualifications and learners belonging to low socio-economic groups, and the opportunities these learners have (if any) towards upward social mobility. For example, except for Tyrone, the remaining learners are either employed by family or in low-paid jobs/casual work or are unemployed.

Learners' school experiences are framed significantly by their academic self-confidence. Learner narratives suggest that school performs a significant role in the personal and academic development of young people, and that experiences of failure, exclusion, and marginalisation can strongly frame learners' future choices and academic self-identities. Furthermore, learners in the study were self-classified as practical at the beginning of their South College trajectories. These self-classifications appear to have been rooted in their GCSE failures and subsequent associations between academic and vocational study. However, over the course of the study, Rachel, Kate, Tyrone, and Abid displayed a shift in their vocational, academic self-concepts and stated a leaning towards theoretical media study. This was particularly prevalent in Kate and Tyrone's case, as these learners progressed onto theoretical or scientific degrees. As the only member of the sample not to continue his studies at South, Dominic reflected a more rapid shift in his academic self-concepts and this was reflected in his chosen pathway.

Although learner identities seemed to shift to reflect their academic trajectories, their earlier experiences of school failure seem to have strongly framed their academic self-conceptualisation. Perhaps the only exception to this was Tyrone, who, unlike the rest of the sample, had experienced sixth-form A Level study. He used the level 2 and 3 media courses as a progression tool to obtain a place on the degree of his choice. It can be argued that Tyrone's subtler experiences of failure did not cause his self-esteem as much damage as the others' did.

By drawing on learners' experiences, it is possible to conclude that their earlier educational experiences at school were damaging to their academic self-conceptualisation. As discussed, in some cases, learners were able to reconceptualise positive academic self-identities over time, while, in others, the damage was long-lasting and affected learners' continued engagement with learning.

Individuals' cyclical relationships with FE

Similarities between staff and learner narratives suggest an ongoing relationship between learners' former FE learning and their self-identities. The staff and I shared similar learning narratives to the learners, returning to FE as practitioners after the sector fulfilled a second-chance role. Positioning this point within the broader context of pedagogy, the question arises as to whether someone who has been through difficult pathways is better placed to support and understand alternatives for students that are going through a period of failure and resettlement in mainstream education. If so, how can such experiences be used to strengthen the FE experiences of failed learners?

Except for Dominic and Kate, the learners demonstrated a sustained engagement with the college. This was surprising in the cases of Richard and Abid, who shared feelings of disaffection and disengagement with their courses, and Tyrone, who had been steered into repeating level 2. What was preventing these learners from seeking opportunities elsewhere, as Dominic had? In Richard and Rachel's case, it is possible to conclude that their long-standing history with the college through their 14–16 engagements had strengthened their connection with the institution.

It can be argued that, in most cases, learners' post-failure encounters with South had enabled connections, whereby the college was identified as a safe space. If this is the case, then when do spaces stop being safe? In Richard's case, South compounded his class barriers and feelings of vulnerability. Yet, even in his disaffection, Richard continued to engage with the institution. Richard's relationship with South College identifies critical issues surrounding learner vulnerability and the role that educational spaces can play in unintentionally enhancing or supporting vulnerability (Ecclestone, 2011).

Navigating marginalised identities

In Richard's case, his low socio-economic status strongly framed his academic narrative. Many of the personal issues that he experienced towards the end of his level 3 studies can be related to his finances and policymaking around the EMA. In essence, how much did the 14-plus framework serve Richard? As his narrative reflects, he perceived himself to be lacking in meaningful media skills and was unable to develop strategies for his dyslexia or independent learning – abilities he was relying on towards the end of his studies at South as he navigated a tricky disciplinary process. Richard's class narrative can be framed as an example of cultural and policy hegemony, and hence raises the question: did South College merely delay the inevitable for Richard?

Except for Dominic, all learners identified as being of low socio-economic status. However, the college was not situated in an underperforming borough nor recognised as supporting learners from underprivileged backgrounds (OFSTED, 2006, 2008). This was reflected in the types of funding and incentives that were available (or unavailable) to the college. Taking these factors into consideration it can be argued that the rhetoric of policy does not consider the nuances of social and class interplay. Perhaps the issue with policy is that its rhetoric generalises too much because, as the young people's experiences have demonstrated, one size of policy does not necessarily fit all.

As Rachel, Tyrone, Kate, and Dominic's narratives suggest, through their persistence, hard work, and resilience, they were able to navigate a problematic learning environment to achieve their aspirations.

There is much to be said about the strength of the individual. Rachel, Dominic, Kate, and Tyrone's narratives reflect the strength that individuals can hold in reconceptualising their life paths. Contrary to the ideology of failed learner classifications, these learners overcame a range of challenges to continue their progression into higher education. If these learners had continued performing the predestined roles that Atkins (2013) presents, it is possible to argue that their life stories may have been very different.

Parity of esteem cultures

This research uncovered new inequalities within the level 2 media in the shape of a lack of parity of esteem between media and other subjects, industry-linked vocational and non-industry linked at the college. These findings can be framed using existing discourse on a parity of esteem between vocational and academic and through the narratives of the learners. In instances such as a lack of parity of esteem between media and other subjects at the college, a broader narrative could be seen at play. However, in most cases, a lack of parity represented a college-specific culture, which in part was interpreting and enacting broader policy discourses. Based on these observations, it is possible to conclude that institutional inequalities can often stem from forms of ideological policy enactment. For example, media education at South was subject to many barriers. Drawing on the case study, these barriers can be identified as:

- Lack of subject knowledge among enrolment staff, resulting in negative effects on learners' recruitment experiences and destinations and departmental learner profiles (consisting of students with limited knowledge of and/or interest in media);
- Issues surrounding the recruitment of appropriate lecturing staff to teach media, thus affecting the quality of learners' experiences;
- Lack of continuing professional development (CPD) and re-skilling opportunities for media lecturers. This point was particularly prevalent in the context of digital developments and changes to specifications. This is reflected in Richard's experiences of peer teaching and Connor's continued lack of CPD;
- Vocational (media) framework shortfalls in relation to learners' lack of industry exposure; and
- A changing and unclear identity for the subject as the college experienced change. This was manifested in its merger with art and the withdrawal of a media-specific middle and curriculum management framework.

These dynamics in South's media department raise concerns regarding the role of media education in FE, bringing into question its long-term value within the current vocational system. This is reinforced by learners' references to the absence of industry experience and links from their vocational media training and questions the currency of their qualifications in industry and the value of the vocational training they are receiving.

Except Dominic, the young people represented creative tendencies, which can be linked to their sustained media study at college. Wider discussion considers the relationship between SpLDs and media study. A study by Tobergte and Curtis (2013) concludes that a high volume of learners with SpLDs are attracted to art or media. Using this framing, it is possible to draw links between Richard and Dominic's SpLDs and their original draw to media. Although learners' enrolment on media was largely serendipitous, possible links between GCSE failure learner types and a creative inclination invites further focus.

As the case study demonstrates, the framing of vocational media as a progression tool is problematic in that it aims to attract learners self-identifying as "practical" and/or those that have previously failed in their schooling. However, this dynamic proves problematic for learners such as Richard, who hold strong aspirations for skilled work in the media industry. Moreover, this positioning also proves problematic for experienced media lecturers in negotiating their identities as subject specialists and FE lecturers. This is evidenced in Tyrone's narrative, which demonstrates an institutional focus on the volume of learners rather than with what has motivated the learner to apply for a media course.

Issues of inclusion

Barriers to inclusion were a salient feature in the narratives of staff and young people. In the case of learners, barriers to their time at South could be identified from their school experiences. Many of the learners shared experiences of exclusionary practices at school. In Dominic, Rachel, and Richard's case, this manifested in their exclusion from the mainstream culture of the school because of their learning disabilities or perceived behavioural issues. As Richard's South College narrative demonstrates, there were close ties between his feelings of similar exclusion at the college and subsequent behavioural issues. Using Richard's narrative, it is possible to cautiously conclude that some schooling cultures may compound learners' feelings of exclusion. This theme also continued into their South College lives, whereby learning support was framed as an additional remedial process that in Richard's case did not enable him with the tools and strategies he needed to manage his condition through learning.

Dominic and Richard's school narratives also reflect a broader issue around the support of students who have learning difficulties. In their narratives, they represent a causal relationship between their SpLDs and exclusionary schooling. The findings suggest that negative schooling attitudes towards disabilities and a lack of support for learners with SpLDs can influence poor GCSE outcomes. Based on Dominic and Richard's narratives, there is also evidence to suggest that some schooling cultures may use SpLD diagnosis as a negative classification tool to define learners as "low ability" or "non-academic".

Class is also framed as a barrier to inclusion for young people in this study. Most learners identified as being of low socio-economic status. It appears that the funding that they would bring in defined their value to the college. This is evident in Richard's college trajectory, which became more challenging once he turned 19 and was no longer able to access financial support from the state. Comparatively, Tyrone's guidance into repeating level 2 did not best serve his academic interests and hindered his natural progression onto level 3 after school.

Barriers to learner inclusion were also visible in the learning experiences of these young people. A decline in teaching quality and access to support reflects a departmental-wide weakened infrastructure, which had negative learning consequences for learners, as Richard, Rachel, Tyrone, and Abid's accounts represent. The support deficit within the department was framed as independent learning and, while Tyrone appreciated his South learning experiences, Richard was made more vulnerable, with negative consequences for his future academic progression.

The barriers were nuanced in the context of staff. The business and marketing rhetoric presented by David sat in tension alongside lecturers' pedagogic identities. Lecturers emphasised values and approaches that aligned with ideologies of integrity, transparency, and opportunity. However, these ideals did not appear to be instilled within the broader culture of South College. David consistently emphasised a college-wide drive for high-quality learning experiences for young people. However, under his leadership, this was not the case for the learners in this study. In practice, learners were often negotiating an uncertain and unstable departmental culture and their learning within it.

Lecturers also experienced barriers to their learning and skills development at South College. As Connor shared, his "deprivation" of CPD was preventing him from obtaining the skills and knowledge he required to be a good media teacher. It is possible to conclude that the lack of opportunities for lecturers' digital upskilling acted as a barrier to their teaching. In an increasingly advanced technological landscape, within which many young people are now identified as "digital natives" (Pelletier, 2005, p. 2), the closing of the skills gap in the vocational media classroom is perhaps more important than ever (Buckingham, 2007; Shah, 2017).

Michael's barriers were two-fold. His earlier school narratives resonated with the negative experiences of young people in this study, as he recalled instances of exclusion based on his dyslexia and negative classifications of being "slow" and, hence, low ability. Secondly, his transition into teaching within the media department also presented barriers. He shared experiences of a divided media team and a lack of support outside of the mentoring he received. It can be argued that Michael's experiences within the media department echo those of some of the learners in this study.

David also experiences barriers to inclusion in respect to college-wide opposition to his decisions and in his broader policy engagement. As David shares, he often had to make difficult decisions that staff did not understand or support. In policy contexts, his lack of inclusion in consultation processes amid an information deficit compounded his feelings of isolation. David's narrative signifies a tension in FE leadership in its mediation of policy and navigation of institutional policy enactment (Fenwick, 2011).

It can be said that David represented progress and change, while the lecturers represented an FE ideology of second chances. This dynamic is reflected in the lack of business acumen the college had previously demonstrated, according to David, in its finance management and college leadership. David emphasised the value of adopting a business model, while Michael and Connor highlighted issues surrounding learning, teaching, and support. In these contexts, it can be argued that David's progress-orientated leadership was alienating experienced teachers like Connor.

This research evidences the complexity and messiness of lived experience and the many contributory factors, drivers, and ecologies that influence the shaping of one's self-identity and lived experience. Most of the young people in this study were able to overcome their barriers to learning and obtain level 3 qualifications. However, Richard's narrative highlights caution to the systemic inequalities that can arise from policymaking and practice. Although colleges like South continued to perform their second-chance FE function, this can often be despite external pressures and rapid policy change.

Recommended discussion topics

- Do you know the prior learning contexts of all your learners? If so, how are you using this information to inform learning, teaching, and support? If not, what mechanisms could be put in place to learn more about each learner context to inform their future learning, teaching, and support?
- What mechanisms could be put in place to elicit sustained learner voice and experience?
- How could learner voice and experience feed into curriculum planning and design?
- What measures could be in place to support teaching teams in delivering specialist applied creative arts provision, such as media studies?
- What mechanisms can be put in place to break down barriers between management and teaching staff?
- How can college enrolment teams be supported in the guidance they give learners?

References

Ainley, P. and Bailey, B. (1997). *The Business of Learning: Staff and Student Experiences of Further Education in the 1990s*. Herndon, VA: Cassell.

Allen, R. and Burgess, S. (2010). Choice and Competition in Education. *Centre for Market and Public Organisation*, (48), p. 19.

Appleby, Y. and Bathmaker, A. M. (2006). The New Skills Agenda: Increased Lifelong Learning or New Sites of Inequality? *British Educational Research Journal*, 32(5), pp. 703–717.

Association of Colleges (2017). *Key Facts College*. London.

Atkins, L. (2009). *Invisible Students, Impossible Dreams: Experiencing Vocational Education 14–19*. Stoke on Trent, UK; Sterling, VA: Trentham Books.

Atkins, L. (2013). From Marginal Learning to Marginal Employment? The Real Impact of "Learning" Employability Skills. *Power and Education*, 5(1), pp. 28–37.

Atkins, L. (2017). The Odyssey: School to Work Transitions, Serendipity and Position in the Field. *British Journal of Sociology of Education*, 38(5), pp. 641–655.

Atkins, L. and Flint, K. J. (2015). Nothing Changes: Perceptions of Vocational Education in England. *International Journal of Training Research*, 13(1), pp. 35–48.

Ball, S. J. (1993). The Teacher's Soul and the Terrors of Performativity. *Journal of Education Policy*, 18(2), pp. 215–228.

Bathmaker, A. and Avis, J. (2005). Becoming a Lecturer in Further Education in England: The Construction of Professional Identity and the Role of Communities of Practice. *Journal of Education for Teaching*, 31(1), pp. 47–62.

Bathmaker, A. M. and Avis, J. (2007). How Do I Cope With That? The Challenge of "Schooling" Cultures in Further Education for Trainee FE Lecturers. *British Educational Research Journal*, 33(4), pp. 509–532.

Bell, L. and Stevenson, H. (2006). *Education Policy: Process, Themes and Impact*. London: Routledge.

Biehl, J., Good, B. and Kleinman, A. eds. (2007). Introduction: Rethinking subjectivity. In *Subjectivity: Ethnographic Investigations*. Berkeley, CA: Berkeley University of California Press. pp. 1–23.

Briggs, A. R. J. (2005). Middle Managers in English Further Education Colleges: Understanding and Modelling the Role. *Educational Management Administration & Leadership*, 33(1), pp. 27–50.

Brown, A. and Pollard, A. (eds) (2006). *14-19 Education and Training: A Commentary by the Teaching and Learning Research Programme*. London: Teaching and Learning Research Programme.

Buckingham, D. (2007). Digital Media Literacies: Rethinking Media Education in the Age of the Internet. *Research in Comparative and International Education*, 2(1), p. 43.

Buckingham, D. (2008). *"Introducing Identity": Youth, Identity, and Digital Media*. Chicago, IL: The John D. and Catherine T. MacArthur Foundation.

Buckingham, D. (2011). Deconstructing Digital Natives: Young People, Technology, and the New Literacies. London: Routledge.

Buckingham, D. (2017). Teaching the Creative Class? Media Education and the Media Industries in the Age of "Participatory Culture". *Journal of Media Practice*, 14(1), pp. 25–41.

Buckingham, D. and Scanlon, M. (2005). Towards a Political Economy of Edutainment Media. *Media Culture & Society*, 27(1), pp. 41–58.

Burgess, M. and Rodger, J. (2010). *14–19 Qualifications Strategy Research*. London: Department for Education (DFE).

Burke, J. (2015). "Not only a car crash, but a multiple pile-up" – the FE sector view revisited six months after the 2015 survey. *FE Week*, [online]. Available at: https://feweek.co.uk/not-only-a-car-crash-but-a-multiple-pile-up-the-view-from-the-sector-six-months-on/ [Accessed 22 April 2022].

Burns, B. J. (2014). 16–18-Year-Olds Achieving A*–C in English and Maths. *BBC News* [online]. www.bbc.co.uk/news/education-29161469 [Accessed 20 May 2022].

Coffield, F., Edward, S., Finlay, I., Hodgson, A., Spours, K., Steer, R., and Gregson, M. (2007). How Policy Impacts on Practice and How Practice Does Not Impact on Policy. *British Educational Research Journal*, 33(5), pp. 723–741.

Collinson, D. and Collinson, M. (2009). 'Blended Leadership': Employee Perspectives on Effective Leadership in the UK Further Education Sector. *Leadership*, 5(3), pp. 365–380.

Corbett, S. (2017). From Teacher to Manager: Expectations and Challenge in the Further Education Sector. A Relationship Model. *Research in Post-Compulsory Education*, 22(2), pp. 208–220.

Dennis, J. (2016). Michael Gove: The Government's Reformer in Chief?. *Pedagogy, Culture & Society*, 1366(July), pp. 1–5.

Department for Business Innovation and Skills (2014). *The Government's Strategy to Support Workforce Excellence in Further Education* (July). Available at: www.gov.uk/government/uploads/system/uploads/attachment_data/file/326000/bis-14-679-further-education-workforce-strategy-the-government-strategy-support-workforce-excellence-in-further-education.pdf [Accessed 9 June 2022].

Department for Business Innovation and Skills (2015). *Progression of College Students in England to Higher Education: BIS research paper number 239*. Project Report. London: BIS.

Department for Children, Schools and Families (2008). *Delivering 14–19 Reform: Next Steps*. Nottingham.

Ecclestone, K. (2011). Emotionally-Vulnerable Subjects and New Inequalities: The Educational Implications of an "Epistemology of the Emotions". *International Studies in Sociology of Education*, 21(2), pp. 91–113.

Elbaz-Luwisch, F. (2010). Narrative Inquiry: Wakeful Engagement With Educational Experience. *Curriculum Inquiry*, 40(2), pp. 263–280.

Elwood, J. (2013) Qualifications, Examinations and Assessment: Views and Perspectives of Students in the 14–19 Phase on Policy and Practice, Cambridge Journal of Education, 42(August), pp. 497–512.

Fenwick, T. (2011). Reading Educational Reform With Actor Network Theory: Fluid Spaces, Otherings, and Ambivalences. *Educational Philosophy and Theory*, 43(SUPPL. 1), pp. 114–134.

Foster, S. A. and Park, S. (2005). *Realising the Potential: A Review of the Future Role of Further Education Colleges*. Annesley: DfES Publications. Available at: http://dera.ioe.ac.uk/5535/1/realising06.pdf [Accessed 9 June 2022].

Fraser, D. M. (1997). Ethical Dilemmas and Practical Problems for the Practitioner Researcher. *Educational Action Research*, 5(1), pp. 161–171.

Fraser, P. and Wardle, J. (2013). Current Perspectives in Media Education: Beyond the Manifesto, *Education Research Journal*, 2011, pp. 74–80.

Frost, N. Nolas, S. M., Brooks-Gordon, B., Esin, C., Holt, A., Mehdizadeh, L. and Shinebourne, P. (2010). Pluralism in Qualitative Research: The Impact of Different Researchers and Qualitative

Approaches on the Analysis of Qualitative Data. Qualitative Research, 10(4), pp. 441–460.

Haynes, G. and Lynch, S. (2012). Local Partnerships: Blowing in the Wind of National Policy Changes. *British Educational Research Journal*, pp. 1–22.

Hayward, G. Hodgson, A., Johnson, J., Oancea, A., Pring, R., Spours, K., Wilde, S. and Wright, S. (2005). *14–19 Nuffield Review 2005–06*. Oxford.

Higham, J. and Yeomans, D. (2006) Emerging Provision and Practice in 14–19 Education and Training: A Report on the Evaluation of the Third Year of the 14-19 Pathfinder Initiative. Nottingham: DfES Publications.

Hill, H., Taubman, D., Hodgson, A., Spours, K. and Wickenden., C. (2012) A Joint Survey by IoE, NUT and UCU on the Curriculum and Qualifications for 14–19 Year Olds: Teacher and Lecturer Perspectives. London.

Hillier, Y. (2006). *Everything You Need to Know About FE Policy*. London; New York, NY: Continuum (Essential FE toolkit series).

Hodgson, A. and Spours, K. (2008). *Education and Training, 14–19: Curriculum, Qualifications, and Organisation*. Los Angeles, CA: SAGE.

Hodgson, A. and Spours, K. (2009). Collaborative Local Learning Ecologies: Reflections on the Governance of Lifelong Learning in England. *Inquiry Into the Future of Lifelong Learning Sector Paper 6*, pp. 1–27. London: Learning and Work Institute.

Hodgson, A. and Spours, K. (2017). FE and Skills Across the UK: The Case of England, pp. 1–11. Available at: www.ucl.ac.uk/ioe/sites/ioe/files/FE_and_Skills_-_the_case_of_England_Final.pdf [Accessed 9 June 2022].

Hodgson, A. Spours, K., Smith, D., Vine-morris, M., Bollam, J., Coles, L., Harris, M., and Kazempour, T. (2017). Education, Skills and Employment in East London: An Ecosystem Analysis. ELVET Programme Research Briefing 1. London: Centre for Post-14 Education and Work, UCL Institute of Education.

House of Commons Education Committee (2011). *Education Committee Participation by 16–19 Year Olds in Education and Training* (July). London: The Stationary Office.

Hyland, T. and Merrill, B. (2003) The changing face of further education: lifelong learning, inclusion and community values in further education. London: RoutledgeFalmer.

James, D. (2002). Transforming Learning Cultures. *Learning and Skills Research*, 6(1), p. 12.

Kirwan, T., Learmouth, J., Sayer, M., and Williams, R. (2003). *Mapping Media Literacy: Media Education 11–16 years in the United Kingdom*. London: British Film Institute.

Kumar, A., Randerson, N. and Kiwana, L. (2013). *The State of Engineering 2013*. London: Engineering UK.

Lingfield, R. (2012) Professionalism in Further Education. Interim Report of the Independent Review Panel. London: Department for Business, Innovation and Skills.

Mehaffy, G. L. (2012). Challenge and Change, Educause Review [online] Available at: https://er.educause.edu/articles/2012/9/challenge-and-change. [Accessed 20 May 2022].

Norton, S. (2012). Potential Realised or Same Old Cinderella? Future Options for England's Further Education Sector. *SKOPE Research Paper*, 109.

O'Connor, J. (2000). The Definition of the "Cultural Industries". *The European Journal of Arts Education*, 2, pp. 15–27.

OFSTED (2006). *College Inspection Report*. Manchester: OFSTED.

OFSTED (2008). *College Report*. Manchester: OFSTED.

OFSTED (2010). *Diplomas: The Second Year*. Manchester: OFSTED.

Opsal, T. D. (2011). Women Disrupting a Marginalized Identity: Subverting the Parolee Identity through Narrative.. Journal of Contemporary Ethnography. doi: 10.1177/0891241610384995.

Pelletier, C. (2005). Studying Games in School: A Framework for Media Education. International Digital Games Research Association Conference. London: Centre for the Study of Children, Youth and Media London Knowledge Lab, pp. 1–12.

Quinney, R. (1982). Nature of the World: Holistic Vision for Humanist Sociology. *Humanity and Society* 6(4), pp. 322–339.

Rose, J. (2012). Building Bridges With Other Schools: Educational Partnerships in Separate Settings in England. *Support for Learning*, 27(2), pp. 84–90.

Shah, J. (2017). Informal learning in a digital landscape: A higher education drama conservatoire case study. In: S. Rutherford, ed., *Informal Learning: Perspectives, Challenges, and Opportunities*. Hauppauge, NY: Nova Science Publishers, p. 314.

Sheerman, B. and Silver, R. (2013). *One System, Many Pathways: Forging Consensus on 14–19 Education and Training*. London: Skills Commission.

Steer, R., Spours, K., Hodgson, A., Finlay, I., Coffield, F., Edward, S. and Gregson, M. (2007). "Modernisation" and the role of policy levers in the Learning and Skills Sector, *Journal of Vocational Education & Training*, 59(2), pp. 175–192.

Thornham, S. and O'Sullivan, T. (2004). Chasing the Real: "Employability" and the Media Studies Curriculum. *Media, Culture & Society*, 26(5), pp. 717–736.

Tobergte, D. R. and Curtis, S. (2013). The 14–19 Diploma: Partnering and Piloting the Agenda Within Higher Education to Enhance and Inspire Future Learners. *Higher Education Academy*, 53(9), pp. 1689–1699.

Tolland, A. M. S. (2016). *Institutional Diversity in the Contemporary Further Education Sector in England*. Unpublished PhD Thesis, University of Sheffield.

Waterman, C. (2011). *Support and Aspiration: A New Approach to Special Educational Needs and Disability*. London: Department for Education.

White, J. (2013). The Coalition and the Curriculum, *Forum*, 52, pp. 1–17.

Wolf, A. (2011). Review of Vocational Education – The Wolf Report. London: Department for Education.

Woodward, K. (2017). Lived Actualities of Cultural Experience and Social Worlds: Representing David Bowie. *Continuum*, 4312(July), pp. 1–10.

Young, M. (2011). The Return to Subjects: A Sociological Perspective on the UK Coalition Government's Approach to the 14–19 Curriculum, *Curriculum Journal*, 22(2), pp. 265–278.

Recommended further reading

Atkins, L. (2009). *Invisible Students, Impossible Dreams*. Stoke on Trent: Trentham Books.

Bates, I. (1985). *Schooling for the Dole?* London: Macmillan.

Esmond, B. and Atkins, L. (2021). *Education, Skills and Social Justice in a Polarising World*. London: Routledge.

Lumby, J. and Foskett, N. (2005). *14–19 Education*. London: SAGE.

Pollard, A. (2004). *The Social World of Children's Learning*. London: Continuum.

Index

Lightning Source UK Ltd.
Milton Keynes UK
UKHW021150290622
405126UK00010B/2010